The Ministry of the Missional Church

The Ministry of the Missional Church

A Community Led by the Spirit

Craig Van Gelder

BakerBooks

Grand Rapids, Michigan

© 2007 by Craig Van Gelder

Published by Baker Books
a division of Baker Publishing Group
P.O. Box 6287, Grand Rapids, MI 49516-6287
www.bakerbooks.com

Printed in the United States of America

Library of Congress Cataloging-in-Publication Data
Van Gelder, Craig.
      The ministry of the missional church : a community led by the spirit / Craig Van Gelder.
          p.   cm.
      Includes bibliographical references and index.
      ISBN 10: 0-8010-9139-X (pbk.)
      ISBN 978-0-8010-9139-1 (pbk.)
      1. Mission of the church. 2. Church work. 3. Community—Religious aspects—Christianity. 4. Holy Spirit. I. Title.
      BV601.8.V28 2007
      266—dc22   2007015763

Permission was granted for use and adaptation of the following sources:

Craig Van Gelder, "From Corporate Church to Missional Church: The Challenge Facing Congregations Today," *Review and Expositor* 101, no. 3 (Summer 2004): 425–50.

Craig Van Gelder, "The Hermeneutics of Leading in Mission," *Journal of Religious Leadership* 3, nos. 1–2 (2004): 139–72.

To all of my students over the years who have continued to challenge and inspire me as we sought together to better understand how to love and serve God

Contents

Figures

Foreword

The Spirit of the Lord fills the whole world
The Spirit of the Lord moves over the deep
The Spirit of the Lord warms our hearts
The Spirit of the Lord fills all things.

Matthew Kelly, *The Rhythm of Life*

This is the invocation for each Wednesday morning in my daily office—it calls us to confess again the source of our lives and the ways God shapes and empowers the church. Scripture tells of God filling us with a new Spirit. In John 20, Jesus appears before his frightened disciples in a locked room, breathes on them the Spirit of God, and creation is reconstituted as the church is born with an identity and mandate to be the sign, witness, and foretaste of where God is moving within all creation. It is in the power of the Spirit that the church receives this mandate, and it is only through the indwelling of the Spirit that the church engages in the ministry of the kingdom. The power of this book is how it is rooted in this recognition and framed by this conviction.

Craig Van Gelder first came onto the screen of my life almost twenty years ago! I was in my second pastorate in Toronto, Canada. It was becoming clear to me as a Canadian that my generation was then far from being called Christian and that most church growth was about the circulation of the saints. It was a time of intense reading and study for me as I searched for ways to frame questions about the place of the church in our culture. I found few in my own context who understood or appreciated the existential nature of my questions about the meaning of Christian life in this strange new world. I was attending a conference one cold May weekend in Chicago that was sponsored by the Seminary Consortium for Urban Pastoral Education (SCUPE). A workshop had a beguiling title about the new missionary situation of the church in North America. I sat in the back of the room listening to Craig talk with deep passion about this theme and was enthralled. I was on a long journey in which my current maps of the territory were becoming more and more useless. I felt lost and alone in a place that didn't make sense anymore. Listening to Craig I knew that, at last, here was someone who understood and could articulate why the maps had failed. He was pointing to ways for us to imagine a different way of being for the church in North America.

Over these twenty years I've come to know Craig as a friend and scholar. I have learned so much from the perspective he brings to the missional conversation. He has an amazing mixture of skills that uniquely equip him to engage the subject of this book. First and foremost, Craig has a passion for the gospel. This is his focus. He's driven to understand the question of what God is doing in the world, and it is not just a polite theological idea. Craig, as you will discover in this book, can bring such a breadth of disciplines and skills to a conversation that you will be amazed at his ability to synthesize complex subjects covering a multiplicity of disciplines. But all this learning is always being used at the service of this one thing—addressing the question of what God is doing in the world. His work is theological and framed by the God question. Hence, this book is an argument for the critical need to understand what the Spirit of God is up to in the world and, therefore, the ways in which the Spirit is seeking to shape the ministry of the church.

A second focus in Craig's writing is the missional church. He is always attending to the meaning and interpretation of a missional theology applied to and engaged with ecclesiology (the questions of what it means to be the church). Craig is immersed in the literature of missional theology and missional church. His lifework is the framing of a domestic missiology for North America. I know of no one who has so consistently followed this commitment in seeking to articulate a thoroughly missional reading of the church. In this book you will find the distillation of this theology and its application for the ministry of the church. This follows from his earlier book *The Essence of the Church: A Community Created by the Spirit*, in which he locates the issues that must be addressed by the church in North America in order to form a missional way of life shaped by the intentions of God.

A third focus of Craig's attention and passion is the local church and the systems that comprise local churches. He brings his learning and skill to the question of what God is doing in and among the people of local churches and the denominational systems that serve them. This book about the ministry of the missional church is for communities of God's people in local contexts that represent a variety of traditions and histories. For those wanting to discover how their traditions and histories have both shaped their story and can become forces in framing missional life, this book offers a comprehensive mapping of how denominations took shape in North America as well as how these traditions can provide important pointers forward.

A fourth focus of Craig's work that is manifest in this book is organizational systems. I know of no other individual in the church world who understands organizational theory and organizational change as does Craig. He has been a consultant to church organizations (local churches, denominational systems, and schools) for many years. He knows the theories and is familiar with all the literature—he owns this field inside the church world. There is no better person than Craig for developing processes for change and innovation from the perspective of the organizational systems of churches and the systems that serve them. As you read through this book you will be introduced to multiple frameworks of organizational life, and you will be provided concrete, practical ways of thinking through how to apply missional innovation in your context. But you will not find this material in the first few chapters. Craig loves the church too much to simply write a book that offers only a set of organizational or management techniques. He knows that the adaptive innovations which are required in our time are about theology, about an imagination for what God is up to in the world, and about what the Spirit is doing in and through the church.

All these foci are woven together in this book. It needs to be read developmentally. Chapter builds upon chapter as Craig creates a map. It begins with an argument for the formation of Spirit-shaped, missional ministry and roots that argument in a biblical framing of God's purposes in the world. These early chapters invite you into a journey of discovery about what the Spirit of God is up to in and through the church in the world. It is from this starting point that you are led into concrete and practical ways to cultivate missional churches. This is an important book: its chapters give you the frameworks and tools to help form missional ministry within multiple contexts. It's easy to write books that offer quick solutions for making the church work. Craig Van Gelder provides an alternative approach by helping you first to frame your world as a leader and then to develop a map for engaging in ministry, a ministry that begins with the important questions about God and moves to concrete proposals regarding the leading of the Spirit.

Alan J. Roxburgh
Director, Allelon Center for Missional Leadership,
Allelon Missional Leadership Network

CHAPTER 1

Spirit-Led Ministry

Alicia was sitting at her word processor, typing a paper for her mission theology class, attempting to bring the ideas that she was working with into a coherent presentation. Then, there it was again, that pesky red underline that appears in Microsoft Word every time a word is typed that is supposedly misspelled. She thought to herself, *Why did the professor keep using the word* missional *in lecturing about mission theology and the church if, in fact, it isn't really even a word?*[1]

A Changing Conversation about the Church

The conversation about the church today is changing. This conversation is introducing a way of thinking about the church that is quite different from several current trends. One such trend is the seemingly endless obsession with trying to discover strategies to help congregations become more effective or successful. These strategies are usually defined in relation to clarifying and carrying out the purpose of the church—the *purpose-driven church*.[2] The necessity of utilizing such strategies is normally justified in terms of the changing context in which the church now finds itself.[3] The church must change and adapt cultural patterns in order to be relevant. Another current trend utilizes the logic of this argument about needing to change in light of a changing context, but offers a different answer as to the solution. This is the *emergent church* discussion where the focus shifts to trying to recapture the ethos and practices of the church of the early centuries and bring these to bear within the emerging postmodern condition.[4]

In contrast to these approaches, a quite different discussion regarding the church also surfaced during the past decade, one that seeks to probe more deeply key questions about the church. It is a discussion that is not being driven primarily by changes taking place in our cultural context, although these are attended to as being important. And it is a discussion that seeks to go beyond just focusing on purpose, strategies, or recovering early church practices. This different conversation is being shaped by a biblical and theological imagination for understanding the very *nature* of the church. The key premise is that understanding the *nature* of the church is foundational for being able to clarify the *purpose* of the church, and for developing any strategies related to that purpose. And understanding the nature of the church is also seen as being foundational for discerning how to address changing cultural contexts. This represents a *change of kind* in the conversation about the church, and is a change of kind being developed around the concept of the "missional church."

The missional church conversation is being popularized largely by the fast-becoming seminal work published in 1998, entitled *Missional Church: A Vision for the Sending of the Church in North America.*[5] This volume is the product of six missiologists who spent two years in intensive discussions attempting to develop a shared argument about the very nature of the church. They sought to explore how the discipline of missiology (understanding God's mission in the world) is interrelated with ecclesiology (the study, *ology*, of the church, *ecclesia*). The result was the construction of a missional ecclesiology, or in short hand, the concept of the "missional church."

This conception of the church is now catching hold among church leaders and congregations across a wide range of denominations. The *missional church* discussion is capturing a basic impulse within many churches in the United States (U.S.) that there is something about the church that makes it inherently missionary. But it is clear that confusion still exists over what the term *missional* really means. Some appear to want to use it to reclaim, yet one more time, the priority of missions in regard to the church's various activities. Unfortunately, this misunderstanding continues the effort to define a congregation primarily around what it *does*. The concept of a church being *missional* moves in a fundamentally different direction. It seeks to focus the conversation about what the church *is*—that it is a community created by the Spirit and that it has a unique nature, or essence, which gives it a unique identity. In light of the church's nature, the missional conversation then explores what the church *does*. Purpose and strategy are not unimportant in the missional conversation, but they are understood to be derivative dimensions of understanding the nature, or essence, of the church. Likewise, changing cultural contexts are not unimportant, but they are understood to be conditions that the church interacts with in light of its nature or essence.

There is a growing literature about the conception of the missional church that is now becoming available.[6] But there is still a need to make more explicit the connections between the church's nature in relation to its purpose and strategies for ministry and also to explore how it engages changing contexts. It is not uncommon for persons to ask, "So, what does a missional church actually look like?" This is a fair question, and to date there has been little research and writing in this area with the exception of the 2004 Gospel and Our Culture series publication *Treasure in Clay Jars*.[7] There is a need to develop a more focused understanding of what Spirit-led ministry looks like in a missional church.

Understanding Spirit-Led Ministry

This volume makes the connection between the church's nature and its purpose in relation to changing contexts more explicit by focusing on the ministry of the church as being Spirit-led. It builds on my earlier book, *The Essence of the Church: A Community Created by the Spirit*, which was published by Baker Books in 2000. That book focused on the nature, or essence, of the church as being inherently missional. In simplest terms, the argument in that volume was developed as follows:

The church is.
The church does what it is.
The church organizes what it does.

The interrelationship of all three aspects is important to understand. *The church is.* The church's nature provides the framework and foundation for understanding the essential character of the church. *The church does what it is.* The nature of the church establishes the foundation for understanding the purpose of the church and its ministry and determines their direction and scope. *The church organizes what it does.* The ministry of the church introduces strategies and processes that require the exercise of leadership and the development of organization within the church.[8] The key point to understand is that the Spirit-led ministry of the church flows out of the Spirit-created nature of the church. What is also critical to understand is that the exercise of leadership and the development of organization need to function in support of this ministry. What is crucial is to keep these in the proper sequence when considering the missional church—nature, purpose/ministry, organization.

The missional church reorients our thinking about the church in regard to God's activity in the world. The Triune God becomes the primary acting subject rather than the church. God has a mission in the world, what is usually referred to as the *missio Dei* (the mission of God).[9] In understanding the *missio Dei,* we find that God as a creating God also creates the church through the Spirit, who calls, gathers, and sends the church into the world to participate in God's mission. This participation is based on the redemption that God accomplished through the life, death, and resurrection of Jesus Christ, a redemption that was announced by Jesus as the "kingdom of God" (which I prefer to reframe as the "redemptive reign of God in Christ").[10] This redemptive reign of God in Christ is inherently connected to the *missio Dei*, which means that God is seeking to bring back into right relationship all of creation. Or as Paul put it in 2 Corinthians, "In Christ God was reconciling the world to himself" (5:19). The Spirit-led, missional church is responsible to participate in this reconciling work by bearing witness to the redemptive reign of God in Christ as good news, and through inviting everyone everywhere to become reconciled to the living and true God.

Seeing the Triune God as the primary acting subject changes the way we think about both the church and the world. The world becomes the larger horizon of God's activity. This represents a fundamental reframing of God's primary location in relation to the world.

When one starts by focusing on the purpose of the church, the church tends to become the primary location of God, which makes the church itself responsible to carry out activities in the world on behalf of God. A trinitarian understanding shifts the focus such that the Spirit-led, missional church participates in God's mission in the world. In doing so, it becomes a *sign* that God's redemption is now present in the world, a *foretaste* of what that redemption is like, and an *instrument* to carry that message into every local context and to the ends of the earth.[11] In living out of this identity and living into this role, the focus for the church shifts primarily to one of discerning and responding to the leading of the Spirit—being a Spirit-led, missional church.

When this understanding is translated to congregations, we find that congregations begin to take seriously how to explore and engage the communities within which they are located. Leadership in congregations focuses on discerning the Spirit's leading and discovering ways to implement ministry in their particular context in light of that leading. Anticipating and accepting change becomes a natural part of the unfolding journey for congregations as they seek to participate in God's mission in their context. Anticipating and addressing conflict constructively becomes a norm in congregational life, since congregations expect differences to emerge in the midst of the changes that are taking place.

The Argument of This Book

Developing this perspective is the purpose of this book. The premise is that it is crucial to understand the Spirit's role in the creation of the church if we are to correctly understand its missionary nature. So also, it is crucial to understand the leading of the Spirit in shaping the church's ministry if we are to correctly understand its purpose. This discussion is developed through the following six chapters.

Chapter 2 provides a biblical framework for thinking more specifically about the ministry of the church in light of the ministry of the Spirit. This chapter examines the ministry of the Spirit throughout the biblical record to identify how the Spirit has worked and is working both in the world and through the church. Patterns of the Spirit's ministry in the Old Testament are examined, the leading of the Spirit in the life of Jesus is defined, and the leading of the Spirit in the life of the early church is explored.

Chapter 3 situates the leading of the Spirit within specific contexts. The church is always located and congregations are always contextual because the church is inherently translatable into any and every context. The challenge is to avoid becoming either undercontextualized or overcontextualized. The key is to understand how the leading of the Spirit is shaping a congregation's ministry as it reads and engages the context within which it is located. This chapter identifies seven inherent aptitudes that a Spirit-led, missional church needs to cultivate in order to minister effectively within its context.

Chapter 4 moves this discussion forward into thinking more specifically about the leading of the Spirit in relation to the church in the context of the U.S. as well as in regard to a more explicit understanding of the missional church. The church has been contextualized and recontextualized within the U.S. over several centuries. It is important to understand something about how the Spirit has led the church over time in this context and how the church's self-understanding has evolved. The fundamental organizational identity of the denominational, corporate form of the church in the U.S. is contrasted with an understanding of the missional church.

Chapter 5 discusses how leadership needs to function within congregations in order to discern the leading of the Spirit and in order to make decisions for developing the church's ministry. This process for discernment and decision making is developed in relation to what is called the "hermeneutical turn." This represents the shift that has taken place in our understanding during the past century that all human knowledge is situated, perspectival, and interpreted. We now see that no one has a privileged position of objectivity when it comes to knowing something. So how then do we proceed to make truth claims? This chapter seeks to answer this question in relation to the role of Scripture in the life of a congregation.

Chapter 6 examines the exercise of leadership and the development of organization within a Spirit-led congregation. It examines how leadership in congregations under the leading of the Spirit can best function in giving direction to a congregation's ministry and in developing organization to support that ministry. These perspectives are developed within an understanding of congregations from an open systems perspective. A variety of insights from the social sciences are utilized to bring further clarity to the functioning of leadership and the development of organization in congregations.

Chapter 7 examines how the ministry of the Spirit leads to growth of and development in the church. This is clearly evident in the Spirit's ministry in the church in the book of Acts. Growth and development in the church also introduce the important issue of change. Some biblical and theological foundations are offered for understanding change as inherent to our being human and being Christian. Various types of planned change are examined along with a process that should be considered when planned change is introduced into the life of a congregation. Attention is also given to understanding the patterns of response that persons often have to change.

CHAPTER 2

Spirit-Led Ministry in the Bible

The weekly Tuesday evening Bible study was meeting at Jim's house, and the six regular attendees were all present. They were discussing Acts 2, which deals with the events surrounding Pentecost. As the discussion began, the topic of conversation soon turned to the ministry of the Spirit.

Bob took the position that just as the Spirit worked supernatural miracles in the days of the apostles, so the Spirit also does today, such as allowing persons to speak in other languages. Jennifer countered this with a question about whether many of the miraculous aspects of the Spirit's ministry hadn't, in fact, ended with the apostolic ministry at the close of the first century.

Sarah interjected that she thought the Spirit's ministry was primarily about bringing individuals to salvation and helping them live holy lives. This was discussed for awhile, and finally James noted that much of the Spirit's ministry in the Bible seems to deal with larger issues about God's people being involved in showing mercy and promoting justice.

Carol wondered out loud whether it was possible to even discern the Spirit's ministry today since so much of it appears to be mysterious and vague. After further discussion, Jim observed that the group needed to spend more time in studying what the ministry of the Spirit actually was as presented in the Bible.

The views expressed by the persons in this Bible study are illustrative of the diversity of perspectives evident in the church today concerning the ministry of the Spirit. Much confusion reigns in the midst of such seemingly contradictory viewpoints. The premise of this book is that it is crucial to understand the *ministry of the Spirit* if we are to comprehend the *ministry of the church* in the world, or more aptly put, how the church is to participate in God's mission in the world. This is a challenge because more attention is usually given to understanding the ministry of Jesus in relation to the church than to understanding the ministry of the Spirit within and through the church.

The majority of the focus historically has been directed toward trying to understand God, in general, and the person and work of Jesus Christ, in particular. Less attention has been given to developing the person and work of the Spirit. This can be seen in the early creeds of the church. For example, in the Apostles' Creed, following fuller affirmations regarding the works of the Father and the Son in the first two articles, we encounter the following line: "And I believe in the Holy Spirit." While the phrases that follow can be associated with the ministry of the Spirit, this is not made explicit in the creed as is the case with the works of the other two persons.

This underdevelopment of the Spirit's ministry is illustrative of what has tended to be the pattern throughout much of the history of the church. What took place during the Protestant Reformation is a good example. At that time, emphasis was placed primarily on developing a Christology—the doctrine of Christ. The Reformers all formulated a theology of the Spirit, but their approaches to the ministry of the Spirit tended to be underdeveloped. A shift in emphasis began to take place in the eighteenth century, however, as a result of the work of John Wesley and the Methodist movement. This growing attention to the Spirit's ministry increased in the twentieth century from a renewed focus by what are known as the Pentecostal, and later, the Charismatic movements.

Today, this increased focus continues in many congregations as they seek to understand the ministry of the Spirit. This often shows up around a discussion of the spiritual gifts, which is an important aspect of trying to understand the Spirit's ministry. But there is much more about the Spirit's ministry that is essential for congregations to comprehend if they are to live fully into all that God intends in relation to God's mission in the world.

Gaining Perspective on the Ministry of the Spirit

Coming to clarity regarding the ministry of the Spirit is an important and challenging aspect of understanding God and the work of the Trinity. There is an abundance of scriptural material about the Spirit. But most of it appears in the biblical narrative somewhat incidentally, more as a subtext within the main text, which is consistent with the person and work of the Spirit. In the Old Testament we find an emphasis primarily on the work of God, in general, and in the New Testament the emphasis is primarily on the work of God the Son. The Spirit's agency is related to the works of the Father and the Son and as such is intended to bring to light their presence and activities in the world. This is also consistent with the teaching about the Spirit in the New Testament, where we find that the purpose of the Spirit is to draw attention primarily to Jesus (John 16:14–15).

The actual appearances of the Spirit in Scripture show up primarily in relation to *specific contexts* and *particular communities* of faith. It is important to attend to the actual working of the Spirit within these contexts and among these communities in order to understand the Spirit's ministry. The practices of the Spirit that are evident provide the raw material for coming to a deeper understanding of the ministry of the Spirit. This approach is referred to as "realistic theology."[1] It takes seriously what is going on within the life of a faith community within a particular context, even while it draws on insights from larger theological frameworks.

Interestingly, those of us in the West now live within a worldview that once again includes an appreciation for spirituality within a dynamic and open universe. This represents a significant shift away from a *closed universe* worldview that became dominant for several centuries under the influence of the Enlightenment.[2] The assumptions embedded in scientific, rational objectivity and logical positivism ruled the day. The biases of these assumptions are now being exposed as a postmodern worldview continues to emerge.[3] In the West, we are in the process of rediscovering spirituality within a dynamic and open universe. In contrast to this, most other societies continued to maintain such a perspective in spite of the influences of modernity. We in the West are also in the process of rethinking theologically the ministry of the Spirit in light of this rediscovery of spirituality within our context.

A Larger Biblical Framework for Understanding the Ministry of the Spirit

The Bible presents the story of God's work in the world in three movements—one that begins with creation, followed by re-creation (redemption) after the fall, and then culminating in a final consummation that introduces a new heaven and a new earth.[4] It is helpful to keep this larger story of the work of God in view when we consider the ministry of the Spirit.

The book of Genesis introduces the Spirit as bringing order out of chaos within the creation (1:2) and being used by God to bring life into existence, life which culminates in the creation of human persons (1:27). The rest of Scripture makes it clear that the Spirit, as the agent of creation, is also involved with the continued well-being of the world.

The Bible conveys that God created both the heavens and the earth. Within this created reality, there were created powers that represent the life forces of existence. These powers, or life forces, are present in human persons and include (a) the desire and need to be in relationship with and to worship the Creator, (b) the desire and need to be in relationship with one another and to create a social community with other persons, (c) the desire and need for men and women to enter into a committed relationship of marriage and produce offspring, (d) the desire and need to engage in meaningful work within the created world, and (e) the desire and need to steward the use of power through engaging in making decisions.[5]

These powers, or life forces, though created good and designed for service to God, became corrupted in the fall. The Bible portrays this fall as beginning with a rebellion against God in heaven by fallen angels and then entering the world as humans also made choices against God. This fallenness leads to the necessity of redemption within the story line, where the Spirit is introduced as the agent of this re-creation. The Spirit is involved in bringing back to right relationship with God that which is fallen. This involves bringing redemption to bear on all of life, both through nurturing the well-being of faith

26

communities and through bringing justice and mercy to bear within the larger world. This role of the Spirit in redemption complements the role of the Spirit in creation. In these roles we find the ministry of the Spirit involved in both the *details of human existence* and the *behaviors of human beings*. There is a material reality to the Spirit's ministry. The Spirit's ministry regularly takes on the particularities of a specific context—e.g., a certain leader, a particular community, or a specific issue or challenge.

The biblical story is brought to its culmination in the final consummation where there is to be the creation of a new heaven and a new earth (Revelation 21–22). It is important to note in regard to the ministry of Jesus Christ that this future has already begun. This is what Jesus refers to as the kingdom of God—or what might be better understood as *the redemptive reign of God in Christ*. The church under the leading of the Spirit is now living between the times—between the *now* and the *not yet*. All the redemptive power of God is already present in the world and is at work in and through the church—the *now*, although sin is still present and its judgment awaits the final consummation—the *not yet*.

The ministry of the Spirit is consistent throughout this biblical story. Various manifestations of this ministry, however, are quite diverse depending on the contexts within which the Spirit's ministry takes place. The scriptural framework presents the Spirit as being *poured out* to become active within the particularities of specific communities of faith and their contexts (e.g., Num. 11:16–30; Isa. 44:3; Joel 2:28; Acts 2:1–4; 10:44). This is also referred to in Scripture on some occasions as the Spirit *descending* (see esp. Matt. 3:16). This pouring out or descending of the Spirit in the Old Testament is often in relation to specific leaders. This is evident as well in the New Testament, especially in regard to Jesus, but the manifestation of the Spirit in the church is usually present in relation to the whole of the church or the corporate leadership of particular congregations.

This pouring out or descending of the Spirit "makes God's power knowable" through creating an intersection between heaven and earth. It brings into play the dynamics of the intent of creation with the possibilities of redemption.[6] As we examine the pattern of the pouring out or descending of the Spirit in the biblical story, we find the following to be present in or to be associated with the ministry of the Spirit:

- demonstrating God's creative power (Gen. 1:2; John 1:1–3)
- affirming God's intention for creation so that all of life might flourish (Gen. 9:1–17; John 10:10)
- confronting the principalities and powers and restraining evil (Gen. 3:15; Eph. 6:10–12)
- reconnecting people and restoring community by helping them come to clarity in their identity as God's people (Genesis 6–8; 1 Peter 2:9–10)
- empowering leadership to guide faith communities into redemptive action (1 Sam. 17:41–47; Acts 19:11–20)
- extending mercy and establishing justice (Isa. 58:6–14; Acts 6:1–6)
- engaging the world (often referred to as "the nations") through witness (Isa. 42:1–9; Acts 1:8)[7]

Dealing with Human Diversity

The Spirit's work within the midst of human diversity in the biblical narrative is related to this larger pattern of the ministry of the Spirit. The reality of human diversity is partially a result of creation design, such as male and female or persons being older and younger. But human diversity is also the result of living within a fallen world where all too often some persons become slaves under the oppression of the free or where enmity is developed between racial or ethnic groups. Such dimensions of human diversity continue to plague human existence in terms of hindering efforts to cultivate reconciled communities. In the biblical story, the Spirit challenges the underlying assumptions and power dynamics often present in regard to human diversity—e.g., views of inferiority, or the oppression and marginalization of certain groups.

The Bible makes it clear that the pouring out or descending of God's Spirit to work in the midst of human diversity introduces a new perspective, which in turn often leads to significant change. This new perspective is that distinctives that divide, or which are used by some to oppress others, take on a different meaning and become relative. We encounter, for instance, the following examples in the biblical record:

Old Testament Examples

- The stranger and the foreigner are now welcome into and protected in the midst of the faith community (Exod. 22:21; Lev. 19:9–10, 33).
- The widow and the orphan are now provided for by the resources of the community (Exod. 22:22; Lev. 19:9–10).
- The poor are to be treated justly and taken care of (Leviticus 25; Isa. 58:7).

New Testament Examples

- A new type of mutuality emerges between men and women and between older and younger (Gal. 3:28; 1 Tim. 5:1–16).
- Slaves and masters are now to treat one another as fellow brothers and sisters in Christ (Gal. 3:28; Col. 3:22–4:1).
- The dividing wall of hostility between Jew and Gentile has come down (Gal. 3:28; Eph. 2:14).

The reality is that some dimensions of human diversity do not disappear, such as gender, age, and race or ethnicity. The ministry of the Spirit does not eliminate these dimensions but rather creates a new kind of relational unity in the midst of these diversities. This unity does not insist on or expect uniformity, but rather it celebrates the dimensions of diversity, redeeming and reckoning them as gifts to be explored. But other aspects of human diversity, such as social status and economic well-being, go through change as the community engages in new relationships of mutuality. Here the ministry of the Spirit invites all persons involved to undergo change in helping to nurture a more holistic expression of human community. For example, masters and slaves coming to see each other as brothers and sisters in Christ was but the beginning of a profound social transformation introduced into the world within and through the Christian community.

This larger framework for understanding the ministry of the Spirit is helpful to bear in mind in approaching the biblical narrative. It provides perspective in helping us discern the broader implications of the specific actions of the Spirit in particular contexts. It also provides perspective in being able to see beyond the human weaknesses we frequently encounter. The bottom line is that the ministry of the Spirit is able to transcend human limitations and failures in bringing about God's redemptive purposes.

The Ministry of the Spirit in the Old Testament

It is fascinating to examine the ministry of the Spirit in the Old Testament. We find the presence and activity of the Spirit involved in every phase of the unfolding story.

The Spirit in Relation to Creation

We are introduced in the creation account to the ministry of the Spirit in the opening narrative of the Bible. The primary word used for the Spirit in the Old Testament is *ruach*, which can also be translated as "wind" or "breath" in addition to "Spirit." It represents an invisible and irresistible power that is present in the world (Gen. 8:1; Exod. 10:13; 14:21; Num. 11:31). The Spirit is encountered in two significant ways in the creation story.

First, we are introduced to the Spirit as the wind or breath of God that moves across the void to bring about order (Gen. 1:2) It is a picture of the Spirit brooding over the chaos, through whose presence the chaos is turned into cosmos. The Spirit is the agent through whom God the Father and God the Son bring all of created reality into existence. This is consistent with the Spirit carrying out the works of both the Father (Gen. 1:2) and the Son (John 1:1–3). All of creation bears the stamp of God's handiwork through the ministry of the Spirit. This includes the created existence of what the Bible refers to as *heaven* or *the heavens*, which represents a spiritual reality. It also includes what we know of as the *earth*, the physical universe.

Related to this creation of heaven and earth, as noted above, are the created powers, the forces of life that shape human existence. These forces of life are the work of the Spirit, which means the Spirit has a proprietary interest in sustaining and preserving the well-being of the whole of creation. The larger horizon of the ministry of the Spirit is

30

always the world. We should therefore expect to see the manifestation of the power and presence of the Spirit sustaining and preserving the well-being of all of creation (Job 33:4; Ps. 104:36).

Second, we encounter the Spirit in the creation account in terms of the "breath of life" that God breathed into Adam (Gen. 2:7). The word used for this "breath of life" is the same word *ruach* that, as noted above, is also translated as "Spirit." Humans created in the image of God (*imago Dei*) bear this image as a distinctive spirituality in relation to the presence of the Spirit (Gen. 6:17; Job 17:1; Ezek. 37:6). While this image was devastated in the fall, it was not altogether lost. Humans still reflect the image of God, although being re-created through the ministry of the Spirit is necessary to realize the full possibilities of what God intended within creation design.

These works of the Spirit in relation to creation and human community represent the two foci of the ministry of the Spirit in the world. The rest of the biblical story unfolds around these realities. God cares about all of creation, desiring to see it flourish. God cares about all persons, desiring to see them reconciled into a right relationship with the living and true God and with one another, even as they take responsibility for the stewardship of all of creation.

The Spirit in Relation to Redemption in the Old Testament

A fundamental problem is introduced into the biblical narrative when we come to Genesis 3. There is rebellion in the spiritual world, i.e., heaven—a rebellion that spills over into the physical world through the sin of Adam and Eve. This reality of sin extends into the whole of created existence. All of life is now disrupted. The relationship between humans and God is broken, so also are the relationships between humans. The created powers, the life forces that were intended that life might flourish, are now fallen. The results quickly become evident in the human community: envy, murder, distrust of one another, blaming, sexual perversion, and human oppression.

The ministry of the Spirit introduces redemption into the midst of the devastation wrought by sin. This redemption is designed to redeem the life forces and to bring back to right relationship that which was lost in the fall. But this is not about going back to the garden. It is rather about looking forward to a future that is yet to come. The horizon of the ministry of the Spirit is still the world. But now the faith community that is to emerge (Israel), while anticipating the future coming of the Messiah, is responsible to bear witness to God's intent to bring redemption to bear on all of life in the world.

It is helpful to examine the variety of ways in the Old Testament in which the ministry of the Spirit is evident within the community of faith and among persons providing leadership within this community. The contexts are often quite different and the circumstances quite varied, but it is the same Spirit that is introducing redemption so that all of life might flourish. There are at least five dimensions to the ministry of the Spirit in the Old Testament narrative.[8]

1. The Spirit empowers God's people with gifts and abilities.

There are times when the Spirit is poured out or descends upon persons for particular purposes in what becomes the co-mingling of the spiritual (theological) with the human (anthropological). These Spirit-infused activities cover a wide range of what might be called the human skills of life, including:

- providing understanding in the use of human reason (Job 32:8)
- endowments and gifts (Gen. 41:38; Exod. 28:3)
- artistic skills (Exodus 36)
- cunning in war (Deut. 34:9)
- heroic leadership (Judg. 13:25)
- wisdom (1 Kings 3:21)
- religious and ethical insights of poets and prophets (Num. 11:17, 25, 29; 2 Sam. 23:2; 1 Kings 22:24; Ezek. 11:5; Zech. 12:10)

The fact that such human skills are under the domain of the Spirit is consistent with the creation of humankind in the image of God (*imago Dei*). It is the Spirit who not only gives life to humans, but who also provides humans with their natural abilities.

2. The Spirit uses leaders to restore community in the midst of oppression or disruption, sometimes using persons who display significant human failings.

The ministry of the Spirit in the Old Testament is clearly manifest in terms of the Spirit's work in promoting the well-being of human community. This is evident in the book of Judges where God raised up a whole series of leaders to deliver Israel from its enemies and to restore communal identity to Israel as being God's people—e.g., Othniel (3:7–10), Gideon (6:1–6), and Jephthah (11:1–40). The pattern is basically the same in these accounts. The Spirit descends on a particular person, and this person leads the people out of their disarray and oppression into restoring community and reestablishing a clear identity for Israel as being God's people. This represents "an intervention of God's Spirit into the structural patterns of human life," an intervention that is very public and which is also highly political.[9] The basic pattern of the working of the Spirit evident in the period of the judges continues after Israel was given a king. However, here the focus shifts to whether the king adequately sought to serve the living and true God in obedience to God's directions, especially as developed through the covenant legislation (e.g., 1 Sam. 11:6; 16:13; 26:11; 2 Sam. 23:2; 1 and 2 Kings).

It is important to note in this pattern of the Spirit's ministry that the Spirit often worked through leaders who were clearly fallible. An example of this is seen in the person of Samson (Judges 12–16). While he showed evidence of wanting to serve God with his whole heart, he also showed evidence of making some very unwise choices, such as in his marriage (14:1–4). A similar pattern is evident in the life of Saul who became the first king of Israel (1 Sam. 13:8–13). But the good news is that God uses humans in the midst of and oftentimes in spite of their weaknesses and limitations.

3. The Spirit exposes evil spirits and confronts the forces of evil.

The Scriptures indicate that, on occasion, God allowed an evil spirit to work within a particular context. We see this, for example, in Judges 9:23 where "God sent an evil spirit between Abimelech and the lords of Shechem" so that "the lords of Shechem dealt treacherously with Abimelech." Similarly, we find in 1 Samuel 16:14 that "the Spirit of the LORD departed from Saul, and an evil spirit from the LORD tormented him." What is important to note about these and similar occurrences is that those in power are the ones who become misguided in coming under the influence of an evil spirit. Related to these occurrences, we also find a regular pattern of prophets who said they were prophesying on behalf of God but who were completely misguided (Jer. 14:11–16).

Typically, it was someone from the margins, one who was often harshly mistreated by those in power, who spoke on behalf of God in confronting the leaders who controlled the dominant political group (1 Kings 22:13–36; Jer. 17:19–33). The ministry of the Spirit in these settings, working through a suffering minority voice, exposed the evil spirits and confronted the forces of evil so that God's larger redemptive purposes could be realized.

4. The Spirit uses the faith community to express mercy and extend justice to the oppressed and to open up full access to the knowledge of God to everyone.

One of the interesting aspects of the Spirit's ministry in the Old Testament concerns the practices of extending mercy and exercising justice. God institutionalized these expectations by building them into the law and in making them part of the public cultic service of God, where the priests were responsible to implement them. We find, for example, that mercy and justice are to be extended to the slave (Exod. 21:2–6), the stranger (Exod. 22:20; 23:9), the widow and orphan (Exod. 22:21–24), the poor (Exod. 22:25–27; 23:6), and to persons without power or influence (Exod. 23:1–3). These actions toward such persons represent what Jesus summarizes in his teaching as the fulfillment of the second great commandment—loving your neighbor as yourself (Matt. 22:39).

God's intent was to have a people who lived in reconciled relationship to God and neighbor and who demonstrated the fuller reality of this to a watching world so all the nations might come to worship and serve the living and true God (Josh. 2:8–14). The practices designed to express this always had the larger world as their primary horizon (Gen. 12:1–3). But these practices also anticipated the eschatological future as part of their ultimate purpose (2 Sam. 7:15–17). They looked toward the type of community that would be created by the Spirit through the coming of the Messiah, as clearly foretold in the messianic passages (e.g., Isaiah 11, 42, 61). Extending mercy, exercising justice, and opening up access to the full knowledge of God to all the nations are part of what it means to be a Spirit-led community of God's people.

5. The Spirit reveals the promised Messiah and the hope of the eschatological future.

The Spirit's ministry in the Old Testament worked to preserve and promote the well-being of human community. But, as noted above, the redemptive purposes of God also looked beyond Israel to a new type of human community that would be formed through the pouring out or descending of the Spirit. This was articulated most clearly within the prophetic tradition, although its theme is part of the story of redemption that is developed throughout the whole of the Old Testament.

Moses, following the pouring out of the Spirit on the seventy elders (Num. 14:14–17), anticipated this in his prophetic statement where he expressed his desire that all of God's people would be able to speak as prophets (v. 29). God's relationship to Israel as a nation anticipated God's relationship to spiritual Israel as the church. In the Old Testament there were manifestations of the Spirit within the nation that came at particular times to particular people. In the church, there would be the manifestation of the Spirit on all believing persons. This theme was picked up by various prophets. Jeremiah developed this around the concept of the new covenant that God would make with God's people (31:31), where the law would be written on their hearts. Isaiah anticipated this in a series of messianic passages foretelling that the promised Messiah would come from the shoot of Jesse (11), would be a suffering servant (42), and would pour out the Spirit on all flesh (61). Joel gave expression to this as well, and his prophecy was picked up by Peter to explain what was happening at Pentecost (Joel 2:28–32; Acts 2:14–21). Ezekiel envisioned this in terms of life being breathed back into dry bones (37:7–10).

These various aspects of the ministry of the Spirit make the work of the Spirit clear in relation to both creation and redemption as these movements unfold throughout the panorama of Scripture. They are under the domain of the Spirit. They operate within the concreteness of specific contexts and the particularities of human behavior. They have a horizon of looking to the well-being of the world. But they also have a horizon of looking toward the fuller revelation of God and the formation of the church to participate fully in the mission of God in the world.

The Ministry of the Spirit in the New Testament

The ministry of the Spirit is introduced in the New Testament in Jesus's birth narratives in the Gospels. The primary word used for spirit or Spirit in the New Testament is *pneuma*, which, parallel to the word *ruach* in the Old Testament, can also be translated as "wind" or "breath" in addition to "spirit" or "Spirit." The ministry of the Spirit in the New Testament becomes much more explicit and detailed than it was in the Old Testament. Jesus provides a specific name for the Spirit as the "advocate" or "helper"—literally a "paraclete" (John 14:16–26). In addition, he clarifies that the ministry of the Spirit would function in the soon to be formed Christian community around the roles of *leading* and *teaching* (John 14:16–17; 15:29; 16:13).

These roles became evident in the book of Acts, as the Spirit led the church into the world and continued to teach the church in the process. Associated with these roles were a wide variety of ways in which the Spirit became identified in the various letters of the New Testament. We find the following phrases in addition to the use of both "Spirit" and "Holy Spirit": "Spirit of your Father" (Matt. 10:20), "Spirit of his Son" (Gal. 4:6), and "Spirit of Jesus" or "Spirit of Christ" (Acts 16:7; Rom. 8:9; Phil. 1:19; 1 Peter 1:11). These various names all indicate the close relationship that the Spirit has with God the Father and God the Son in the ministry that the Spirit carried out. This becomes clearly evident in the Gospel narratives when we examine the life and ministry of Jesus.

The Spirit and Jesus in the Gospels

The story of Jesus as presented in the four Gospels demonstrates that the horizon of redemption envisioned in the Old Testament was now coming to fulfillment. The Gospels make it clear that the ministry of Jesus was bringing this redemption into being under the leading of the Spirit. This reflects how the work of the Spirit is always carried out in relation to the works of both the Father and the Son. The Spirit is involved in every aspect of Jesus's life and ministry from conception to ascension. This anticipates what becomes the leading of the Spirit in the life and ministry of the church as the body of Christ in the world.

1. The Spirit was involved in the birth of Jesus.

The events surrounding the birth of Jesus take place under the leading of the Spirit. Even while John the Baptist was in his mother's womb, it was foretold that he would be filled with the Spirit (Luke 1:15, 80). Mary was informed by an angel that she would conceive the Son of God by the Holy Spirit (1:35). Elizabeth was filled with the Holy Spirit in welcoming her cousin Mary who was now with child (1:41). Zechariah was filled with the Spirit in prophesying about the Savior to be born following the birth of his son who became John the Baptist (1:67). At Jesus's birth, Simeon, under the leading of the Spirit, divined the presence of Jesus and worshiped him (Luke 2:25–32). All these activities of the Spirit made it clear that there would be a very close relationship between the leading of the Spirit and the life and ministry of Jesus.

2. The Spirit was involved in the life and ministry of Jesus.

Similar to the birth of Jesus, the events relating to the life and ministry of Jesus also take place under the leading of the Spirit. We find John the Baptist explaining that in contrast to his baptism with water, Jesus would baptize with the Holy Spirit and fire (Matt. 3:11; Mark 1:8; Luke 3:16). When Jesus was baptized, the Spirit of God descended on him like a dove (Matt. 3:16; Mark 1:10; Luke 3:22).[10] Following his baptism, Jesus returned from the Jordan River full of the Holy Spirit and was then led by the Spirit into the wilderness to face the forty days of temptation (Matt. 4:1; Mark 1:12; Luke 4:1). Jesus made it clear in his early teaching that one had to be born of the Spirit in order to know God (John 3:5–8).

Following John's arrest, Jesus, filled with the power of the Spirit, returned to Galilee to begin his public ministry (Luke 4:14). Jesus announced in the synagogue at his home town of Nazareth that the Spirit of the Lord was upon him as he proclaimed the fulfillment of Isaiah 61 (Luke 4:18–21). When Jesus instructed the apostles before sending them out two-by-two, he informed them not to worry about what to say, for the Spirit of their Father would speak through them (Matt. 10:20). After receiving the report from the seventy following their return from their missionary work, Jesus rejoiced in the Spirit, giving thanks that God was revealing such things to them (Luke 10:21). Jesus made it clear that the Holy Spirit is the greatest gift the Father can give to God's people (Luke 11:13). Jesus also made it clear that King David had spoken of him by the Spirit in calling him "Lord" (as recorded in Psalm 110:1).

3. Salvation was introduced in all its fullness through Jesus's life and ministry.

Throughout his ministry, Jesus confronted the principalities and powers and defeated the presence of evil. We find him casting out evil spirits on many occasions, pointing out on one occasion that he did so by the power and presence of the Holy Spirit (Matt. 12:18). He regularly confronted the religious authorities who oppressed the people and offered the poor and the marginalized in society redemptive hope in being part of a new type of community (Matt. 5:1–16; Luke 6:20–38). He consistently addressed the brokenness of life through many of the miracles that he performed, especially in healing the sick (Mark 1:34). He occasionally challenged the forces of nature in such acts as quieting a storm (Matt. 8:26), walking on water (Mark 6:47–51), and raising the dead (Mark 5:35–43).

All of these aspects of his ministry were performed in the power of the Spirit, and all of them brought fulfillment to the Old Testament expectation regarding the salvation that was to be realized in the coming of the Messiah. The redemptive power of the eschatological future was now evident in the person and ministry of Jesus—the manifesting of the kingdom of God. This reign of God in Christ represented a *force field* of the power and presence of God's redemptive work in the world.[11] This force field of redemptive ministry was the clear manifestation that the Spirit of God was present (Matt. 12:22–30; Luke 11:14–23).

4. Jesus promised the ministry of the Spirit in the church.

At the end of his public ministry, Jesus made it clear to his disciples that he was going to leave them, but he was not going to leave them alone. He promised that when he returned to the Father, he and the Father would send the Spirit to be with them. As mentioned earlier, Jesus refers to the Spirit as an "advocate" or "helper"—literally a "paraclete" (John 14:16–26). This Spirit would lead them and teach them. The same Spirit that led Jesus throughout his life would also lead the church in all of its life and ministry. As this ministry unfolded, it would involve the Spirit convicting the world of sin, righteousness, and judgment (John 16:8)—a ministry which began to become manifest at Pentecost (Acts 2:37).

Jesus is called and sent by the Spirit to participate fully in accomplishing God's mission in the world. So also, the church is called and

38

sent by the Spirit to do the same. This includes (a) the continued stewardship of all of creation, (b) making redemption available to all persons, (c) bringing redemption to bear on every aspect of life, and (d) forming a faith community to carry out these ministries. It is interesting to study the emergence of the church in the rest of the New Testament to gain perspective on the ministry of the Spirit.

The Spirit in the Book of Acts

The kingdom of God as announced by Jesus, i.e., the redemptive reign of God in Christ, clearly anticipated that there would be a community of believers built up around the twelve apostles who would carry the message of the good news about the kingdom to the world (Matt. 28:18–20). Jesus did not provide a lot of specific content about how this community of believers would be organized and how it would function, but Jesus made it evident that the Spirit's presence within this community and the Spirit's working through it would make this new organization unique in the world.

They would be empowered by the Spirit, doing even greater things than Jesus himself had done during his public ministry (John 14:12). They would be taught by the Spirit, learning how to discern the leading of God and the working of God's redemptive purposes within particular contexts (John 14:26). They would be led by the Spirit into the world and empowered to participate fully in God's mission, which Jesus identified as beginning with the announcement to the world of the forgiveness of sins (John 20:21–23). And they would be responsible to carry this good news to the ends of the earth (Acts 1:8).

The book of Acts is a natural starting point for gaining insight into the ministry of the Spirit. It could just as readily be entitled *The Acts of the Spirit* as *The Acts of the Apostles*. References to the presence of the Spirit are abundant. We find the Spirit mentioned over forty times, where the ministry of the Spirit is manifest in the following ways:

- The *Spirit spoke through Old Testament authors* (Acts 1:16; 2:17–18; 4:25; 28:25).
- The *Spirit is poured out* on believers (Acts 1:8; 2:1–4; 2:33; 5:32; 10:38; 10:44–47).

- Believers *receive the Spirit* and are converted (Acts 2:38; 9:17; 19:6).
- Believers were *filled with the Spirit* (Acts 4:8; 4:31; 6:3, 5; 7:55; 11:24; 13:9; 13:52).
- The *Spirit spoke through certain persons* (Acts 6:10; 10:19; 21:4, 11).
- Some persons *opposed or lied to the Spirit* (Acts 5:3, 9; 7:51).
- The *Spirit directed decisions or actions* (Acts 8:29; 8:39; 13:2–4; 15:28; 16:6–7; 21:4, 11).
- The church was *comforted by the Spirit* (Acts 9:31).

Acts provides an account of what the followers of Jesus experienced after the Spirit was *poured out* upon them. The author structures this book around the Spirit's activities of ensuring that the gospel would be taken to everyone, all the way to the ends of the earth, and that it would address all of life—*everyone, everywhere, everything.* Jesus had made it clear that this was God's intent (see Matt. 28:19–20; Acts 1:8). This should have introduced the regular activity of employing *wisdom and planning* for this purpose in the life of the early church. However, the church struggled to bring this intent of God into their shared practices. This led to new voices, often from the margins, calling for *faith and discernment* to understand the working of the Spirit in leading the church into the world (e.g., the first missionaries being sent out from the church at Antioch).

Under the Spirit's leading, and oftentimes in spite of the church's reluctance, the gospel continued to cross boundaries and become contextualized within new cultural settings. This demonstrates that the church is always *forming*, even as it seeks to also be *re-forming*. The ministry of the Spirit in the book of Acts makes a direct connection between the sharing of the good news about Jesus with three results: (1) the spreading of the gospel message, (2) the growth and development of the church, and (3) the influence of the gospel and the growing church within various cultural contexts. This is consistent with the vision for the ministry of the Spirit in the Old Testament. We find regular references to growth and development taking place, both in terms of people coming to faith in Christ—*evangelizing*, and in regard to the broader redemptive influence of the gospel coming to bear on social and cultural realities—*mission*.

This ministry of the Spirit in relation to evangelizing and mission anticipates the continued expansion of the church throughout the ages. Acts ends with the Word continuing to be proclaimed by Paul in Rome as a witness to this expectation (Acts 28:30–31). The presence of the Spirit and the Spirit's teaching and leading the church give birth to a church that is missionary by nature. The Spirit-led church's very existence in the world has to be understood in missionary terms. The church cannot help but participate in God's mission in the world. This is part of what it means to be the church. To do less would be contrary to its nature. While we find that the church in its history has at times not fully understood, or lived out of this reality, the Spirit's presence in the church means that this reality is always there to be cultivated and lived into.

The Spirit in Relation to the Church

The ministry of the Spirit in relation to the church begins to unfold in the book of Acts and is further developed in the various letters that make up much of the rest of the New Testament. Taken together, these sources provide a substantive presentation of how the Spirit is involved with the church. There are at least five dimensions of the Spirit's ministry that can be identified, all of which are consistent with the ministry of the Spirit that is evident in the Old Testament as well as those that come to expression in Jesus's ministry.

> 1. The Spirit creates a new type of reconciled community through accomplishing redemption and gives this community a new identity as the church of Jesus Christ.

The letters of the New Testament make it clear that the Spirit is the agent that brings salvation to bear in the lives of persons in justifying them by grace through faith. This is the result of the love of God being "poured into our hearts through the Holy Spirit" (Rom. 5:1–5). So also, it is the Spirit who serves as the seal of the assurance of this salvation, where the Spirit "is the pledge of our inheritance toward redemption as God's own people" (Eph. 1:13–14). It is important to note here the *pouring out* of the Spirit into the lives of believers, similar to what was foretold in the Old Testament and seen in Acts. It is also important to note that the emphasis is on God creating a people, a redeemed community, as a result of the Spirit's work. The church is created as a community into which individuals are incorporated, rather than being a community that is constructed by self-selecting individuals (as understood by modern, Western social contract theory in relation to volunteerism).

The type of community that the Spirit creates consists of reconciled diversity. This is given its clearest expression in Galatians 3:28, although similar points are made in Ephesians 2 with the breaking down of the wall of hostility and the creation of one new humanity (vv. 14–15). In Galatians, we find that when we are baptized into Christ, then there is no longer Jew or Greek, slave or free, male or female. There is, in fact, a new kind of oneness that now exists in the midst of these former diversities. It is important to note that two of these diversities are inherent (ethnicity and gender), while the other is socially constructed (social-economic status). As pointed out earlier, the presence of the Spirit cuts across both types of diversity in creating a new perspective with which to view the *other*. It is important to note here that other passages in the New Testament provide more explicit instructions regarding how this latter constructed diversity is to be seen. For example, Paul invites Philemon to receive back Onesimus, his former slave, now as more than a slave, in fact as a "beloved brother . . . both in the flesh and in the Lord" (Philemon 16). Communities of reconciled diversity are God's intent in regard to the ministry of the Spirit. This has profound implications for congregations in the U.S. context, where market forces and socioeconomic realities tend to drive us into communities of homogeneity.

2. The Spirit gives and empowers leadership to guide these communities.

It is also a part of the Spirit's ministry to provide these communities of reconciled diversity with leadership. Evidence of this is found in Acts 6, where we find the Spirit involved in the selection of the seven persons who were to assist in providing leadership in the early church in Jerusalem. So also, we find the Spirit separating Barnabas and Paul out from among the leaders in the church at Antioch to be sent out for cross-cultural ministry in the Greek provinces of Asia

Minor. Similarly, we find Paul exhorting the elders from the church in Ephesus to keep watch over the flock given them by God, since the Holy Spirit had made them "overseers to shepherd the church of God" (Acts 20:28).

These experiences of the church in Acts are consistent with the teaching that Paul provides in 1 Corinthians regarding the gifts of the Spirit and the role of leadership in the church. We find that there are a variety of spiritual gifts that the Spirit gives to the church, all of which are intended for the common good (12:7–11). In the midst of teaching about these gifts, however, we also find Paul noting that some of the gifts given are *gifted persons* who provide leadership—"first apostles, second prophets, third teachers" (12:28). These Spirit-gifted gift-persons are to provide leadership in the church for the benefit of the whole. This understanding of Spirit-gifted gift-persons is also found in Ephesians 4 where the focus is on these persons equipping all of God's people (the saints) to become involved in Spirit-led ministry (vv. 11–12).

3. The Spirit leads these communities into sanctified living consistent with their new nature in Christ.

Paul makes it clear in Romans 8 that a new way of life is to be enjoyed by those who are in Christ—a new life that is led by the Spirit. The "Spirit of life" has set us free from "the law of sin and death" (v. 2). We are no longer subject to the demands of the flesh, since these were put to death in the death of Christ. This now allows the church to "walk not according to the flesh but according to the Spirit" (v. 4). There is, in fact, a new nature that has been given to the church, one that is the creation of the Spirit where the Spirit of God now dwells in us (v. 9). In light of this new reality of the Spirit's indwelling, the church is invited to "put to death the deeds of the body" (v. 13). It is by the grace given through the Spirit's presence that the church is empowered to do this. This is similar in thought to Ephesians 2:8–10, where we find that as a result of being justified by grace through faith, we have also been created for good works, which is to be our "way of life." To do this, the church must be led by the Spirit. Being led by the Spirit is the mark that we are in fact "children of God" (Rom. 8:14).

We find in Galatians that living in the Spirit and being guided by the Spirit are to be the marks of the church (5:25). Here Paul sets

43

up a similar contrast between the desires and works of the flesh and the fruit of the Spirit. Evidence of the works of the flesh is spelled out: fornication, impurity, licentiousness, idolatry, and the like. Paul notes that because the Spirit has been given to us, we are no longer subject to living by these passions, which results from being subject to the law (v. 18). Rather, in light of the new nature we have been given, we are now free to experience and express the fruit of the Spirit: love, joy, peace, patience, kindness, generosity, faithfulness, gentleness, and self-control. Clearly, the communities of reconciled diversity that the Spirit creates now have not only the responsibility but also the power to live by a different set of values in the world. It is this communal lifestyle that displays contrasting values to those of the world, where this lifestyle serves as the basis for the church having an effective witness in the world.

4. The Spirit leads these communities into active ministry.

As noted earlier, it is the Spirit that is the agent of God who brings the gifts of God into the life and ministry of the church. This is based on the gifting of the church by Christ (Eph. 4:7–8) and manifests itself in each participant in the church being the recipient of the Spirit's spiritual gifts—"to each is given the manifestation of the Spirit for the common good" (1 Cor. 12:7). It is important to note several aspects of the Spirit's spiritual gifts. They all come from the same Spirit (12:11), which means that there is an inherent unity in their presence and in their use in relation to the wide-ranging diversity of their various ministries. They are given to believers based on the Spirit's choosing (12:11). This means that members need to discern and discover their gifts and find their place in the body of Christ in light of this. Paul makes a major point of trying to help the Corinthian church understand that each person and each gift is important, and that believers are, in fact, interdependent with one another. Learning to become mutually interdependent in such a way that all persons and their gifts are honored is an expression of being led by the Spirit (12:14–26).

These gifts of the Spirit are not primarily for the recipients' benefit. Rather, they are given both for the sake of the body and for the sake of the world. As the gifts are exercised in the body, grace flows through the ministries that take place such that persons become "members one of another" (Rom. 12:5), which results in the promoting of the "body's growth in building itself up in love" (Eph. 4:16). As these gifts are exercised by God's people, ministry also becomes manifest in the world (Rom. 12:14–21). The world is always the larger horizon of God's intent and the Spirit's ministry. Spirit-gifted believers living out their lives in the world both collectively and individually bear witness to the redemptive reign of God in Christ as they exercise the gifts of the Spirit and live out of their new nature in expressing the fruit of the Spirit. They become a demonstration to the watching world that God intends that all of life might flourish, and they become God's agents in the world through the leading of the Spirit to help cultivate this reality.

> 5. The Spirit leads these communities into the world to unmask the principalities and powers through a ministry of suffering service.

The church encounters the reality of sin and the brokenness of the world as the Spirit leads the church into the world to participate in God's mission. We find that believers along with creation itself "groan inwardly" as all await the release from the bondage of sin (Rom. 8:18–24). But while the church lives in this in-between time, it also encounters the forces of evil that the Bible refers to as the "principalities and powers" (also translated as "rulers and authorities") (Eph. 6:12). These powers seek to thwart the ministry of the Spirit. However, it is through the church being led by the Spirit into ministry in the world that these principalities and powers come to know the "wisdom of God" (3:10). It is the church being led by the Spirit and in living as a reconciled community of diversity in the world and engaging in ministries of mercy and justice that unmasks these principalities and powers and shows them to be, in fact, without dominion in the world. God in Christ defeated these principalities and powers and showed them to be without ultimate authority (Col. 2:15). Now the Spirit is leading the church into the world to demonstrate this reality by unmasking them through the Spirit's ministry in and through the church.

This ministry of unmasking the powers does not come through triumphalism but rather follows the way of the cross in a lifestyle of suffering service (Rom. 8:14–21). But it is an unmasking that does not go uncontested. There is a real battle between the forces of evil and the presence of God's reconciling grace in the Spirit's ministry through the church in the world (Eph. 6:10–17). In the midst of this battle, however, the church is assured that God is for us (Rom. 8:32). Since God is for us, we are secure in the love of Christ, and there is nothing that can separate us from God, whether "hardship, or distress, or persecution, or famine, or nakedness, or peril, or sword" (8:35). This promise clearly indicates that the church living out a lifestyle of suffering service under the Spirit's leading will not be exempt from such pain and adversity. But this promise also includes the deeper reality that there is nothing, not even the "powers" themselves, that can "separate us from the love of God in Christ Jesus our Lord" (8:39). So the church joyfully enters into ministry in the world to engage in reconciling diversity, extending mercy, and exercising justice, all the time knowing that it will often be misunderstood and mistreated, but also knowing that the grace of Christ is sufficient (2 Cor. 12:9).

Summary

The ministry of the Spirit pervades the whole of Scripture but usually comes to expression more as subtext than text. This is the nature of the Spirit's work, i.e., to carry out the works of God and bring glory to the person of Christ. It is critical for the church to understand the ministry of the Spirit if it is to understand how to participate fully in God's mission in the world. Attending to the ministry of the Spirit provides the framework for understanding this participation. This framework represents the focus of the rest of this book, where the ministry of the Spirit is examined in relation to congregations in the context of the U.S.

CHAPTER 3

Spirit-Led Ministry in Context

First Church recently celebrated its one-hundreth anniversary in serving as the only congregation of its denomination in the small, farming community of Russellville. The established white population of the community was continuing to decline, but interestingly, new growth was occurring in the area both from recreational development taking place at the nearby lake and from Asian immigrants who were taking jobs at the local turkey processing plant. Active members at First Church now numbered about eighty-five in worship, but the average age was sixty-five. It was becoming clear to the leadership that the congregation would likely experience significant decline in the next decade due to deaths, unless new persons could be reached. What strategy should they pursue?

St. Luke's was a first-ring suburban congregation facing significant ethnic changes in its immediate neighborhood where many of its original members once lived. Most of the new residents were recent immigrants from Central and Latin America. This made the challenge of relating to the newcomers even more difficult for the members of St. Luke's due to language as well as ethnic and cultural differences. For an extended period of time, there was mostly denial at St. Luke's that things had really changed. But with a significant loss of membership over the past five years, the leadership was beginning to recognize that something needed to be done. They had few clues, however, regarding how to proceed. What strategy should they pursue?

New Life Community was a twenty-year-old congregation built around a seeker-friendly strategy that sought to attract primarily persons from among the late baby boomers (born in the mid-1950s into the 1960s). It grew to over 3,200 active worshipers during its short history, with this substantial growth requiring what seemed like constant change in leadership practices and organizational design. But now it was facing a different kind of change. The leadership recently began to track more carefully its growth patterns and realized that they were not reaching the next generation. It appeared that their basic model for ministry was largely generation-based around the late boomers. What strategy should they pursue?

The experiences of these congregations are typical of what thousands of congregations are encountering today. Contexts go through fundamental change, which require congregations to consider how they might respond. The tendency is to approach the challenge of contextual change primarily from the perspective of developing strategies. But unfortunately, the strategies employed by many congregations often tend to be either too late in response or too limited in scope. Congregations that successfully adapt to such fundamental change are few. Even those that are successful usually end up having their core identity substantially challenged and eventually changed. This often occurs largely by default rather than by design. It is the premise of this book that in the midst of this process of constant change taking place within congregational contexts a congregation needs to understand the ministry of the Spirit. God's intent often is to use such change either directly or indirectly to move a congregation in new directions of meaningful ministry under the leading of the Spirit.

Contexts Are Always Changing

It is critical for congregations to realize that contexts are always changing. This is the very nature of life. Congregations would be well served by staying on the front side of the curve in anticipating contextual changes so they could intentionally continue to recontextualize their ministries to address new conditions as they emerge. Unfortunately, this is all too often not the case.

The process of change taking place in congregational contexts can vary in both scope and speed. Some contexts tend to change slowly over a long period of time, such as through the natural aging cycle of a community. Other contexts go through rapid change where everything seems to be impacted, such as experiencing a turnover in the ethnic composition of the population. Congregations need to be prepared to address either type of change.

Some contexts change incrementally over time. Change in the context of most congregations until recent decades was usually incremental, being experienced over extended periods of time. This allowed for substantial continuity in ministry patterns and organizational forms over a period of several decades or in some cases over several centuries. But for many of these congregations, even though they were able to function for long periods of time with relative stability, the cumulative effects of incremental changes finally catches up with them.

The image is familiar to most of us of the small town church with its over a hundred-year-old building located just off of Main Street, as illustrated by the example of First Church in the opener. The average age of the majority of such congregations today is sixty years and up, usually due to children continuing to leave the community over the years. What is not so readily evident is that many of these seemingly dying congregations are located in communities where significant numbers of new persons are moving in. This is occurring in many rural areas due to retirement and recreation opportunities. It is also occurring in many rural areas where persons of color have moved in who are willing to take low-wage jobs in area agriculture and livestock processing plants. On the surface such congregations appear to be in inevitable decline and a slow death. In reality, new opportunities for mission and ministry await their engagement. The challenge is to act early enough while resources are still available to engage in such ministry. The failure to recontextualize ministry while incremental changes are taking place ultimately takes its toll with most of these congregations. They eventually either close or merge with other dying congregations.

Some contexts change dramatically. There are times in the life of the church when change is quite interruptive, where it occurs in a tumultuous manner. This is referred to as discontinuous change.[1]

This type of change always brings substantive disruption into the life of a congregation, although there may be a delayed response to such a change by the congregation. There may be some early indicators that such changes are going to take place. But few congregations are prepared to read these signs in time to implement effective strategies to recontextualize their ministries. They usually end up reacting to the change, making inadequate adjustments long after the opportunity to connect with new people moving in has been lost.

Changes made in immigration policy by the U.S. during the 1960s and 1970s allowed for a significant inflow of persons from Africa, Central and Latin America, and the Pacific rim. Many of the persons immigrating from these regions settled in urban areas during the past few decades, as illustrated in the example of St. Luke's in the opener. Substantial changes in the composition of the population of many neighborhoods and communities along ethnic-racial lines are continuing to take place all across the country. Many of the congregations that were developed to serve a predominately Anglo population now face the challenge of serving multicultural communities. Most of these congregations are struggling to respond. While congregations have the biblical mandate to recontextualize their ministries in such rapid times of change, few are able to do so. Of those that do, there are usually significant levels of disruption and pain.

Another way of experiencing rapid, discontinuous change is illustrated in the example of New Life Community. This is a church that is not tied to any particular neighborhood. It built its life around ministering to a specific population segment: late baby boomers. Changing cultural patterns between generations, however, are now making their ministry model obsolete for reaching the next generation. It will be difficult for them to make significant shifts in their ministry model without challenging their core identity, which has been built around the cultural preferences of a particular population segment.

Change as both helpful and harmful. Change is a mixed reality. There are many cases where contextual changes, although initially disruptive, can actually benefit congregations and their ministries. The migration of persons from other ethnicities into the broader community that a congregation serves can actually invite a congregation to develop a missional imagination for serving and reaching the *other*.

The message of the Bible is that God is a God of hospitality who is always inviting his people to welcome the stranger or the foreigner that comes into their midst. A Spirit-led congregation is reminded that they also were once strangers and foreigners and that they can actually grow into a deeper understanding of the reconciling power of the gospel as they become relationally connected to the *other*. The biblical and theological issue is that cultural diversity needs to be understood as a gift from God to be celebrated rather than as a problem to be solved.

There are some changes in the context around a congregation, however, that can be profoundly difficult to respond to or even harmful. A natural disaster that hits a community, such as a flood or tornado, is often devastating to the well-being of human life and disruptive of congregational life. Dramatic changes in the local economy brought on by the closing of a plant by a major employer can have devastating effects on a congregation. Likewise, changing social values that challenge biblical understandings of morality in terms of marriage, divorce, and sexuality can be quite challenging to a congregation as it seeks to maintain its own identity while responding to persons in the community it serves.

So change needs to be assessed carefully to discern whether it is helpful or harmful. This is a continuous task for a congregation that is seeking to be Spirit-led in being faithful to the gospel in its context. This is especially so for a congregation that is seeking to recontextualize its ministry in relation to changes that are taking place. Congregations are now finding themselves at the beginning of the twenty-first century at a significantly different location than just a few decades ago as they continue to experience and live into the emerging postmodern condition.[2] It is helpful to note more specifically the variety of ways in which congregations attempt to respond.

Responses to Changing Contexts

What is it about the church that allows it to be so creative and innovative in seeking out new opportunities for ministry on the one hand and yet so reactive and resistant to change on the other hand? How are we to understand these dimensions as being part of the same church of Jesus Christ? It is interesting to examine some of the strategies that congregations use in responding to changes taking place in their context. There are several approaches.

Relevance. Typical of many congregations is a strategy of seeking to incorporate new elements of the emerging cultural patterns into their ministries. This is a helpful instinct to pursue in terms of working at recontextualizing a congregation's ministry as changes take place. However, this strategy can become problematic when it leads to a kind of faddishness. This is evident today among many congregations that are always seeking after what might be called the "new and the next"[3]—e.g., adding a contemporary worship service, creating projection capability in the auditorium, moving to a spiritual gift–based deployment process, and so on.

Congregations pursuing such strategies are seeking new ways of doing church as they adapt yet one more time to the changing culture. This pattern is especially typical of many of the generation-targeted church planting strategies that have become popular in recent decades. Such efforts to be relevant are shaped largely by a congregation's pragmatic desire to become effective and successful. Congregations often pursue this desire by drawing on the experiences of successful models, even though these exemplary congregations usually warn others against trying to do so. The most popular and influential current examples of this approach are provided through the various conferences sponsored by Willow Creek Community Church and Saddleback Church.

The tendency is to look for methods that work or to find models of ministry that can be applied in different locations. Most of these efforts are filled with good intent and usually are informed by biblical perspectives. But they often fall short of becoming adequately grounded in solid biblical and theological foundations. Also, they often fail to take into consideration insights from the historical Christian faith that could help guide them in responding to their changing context. For example, we now find generational, multicongregational congregations that segment the population around particular age groups. Lost in this strategy is something about the intergenerational nature of Christian community and insights into the faith that come from diversity being part of the makeup of God's people.

Resistance. Many congregations, in the face of significant change in their contexts, try to stave off the change through strategies of resistance. While this impulse can be helpful up to a point, depending on the changes that are taking place this approach often takes on a reactive character. Typically, efforts are made to maintain the status quo or even, at times, to recover a former approach to ministry from another historical time. For example, some congregations continue to stress strict adherence to particular confessional standards as being the true interpretation of the faith. A quick read of church ads in the yellow pages in most cities illustrates that this is often the primary way such congregations convey (market) their image to those located in the context they seek to serve. For example, Trinity Lutheran—A Biblical, Traditional, and Liturgical Lutheran Church, or Fourth Reformed—A Congregation that Stands True to the Historic Confessions.

Such congregations seek to maintain their ministries by defining themselves over against other congregations that are perceived as having departed from the purity of the faith. Their stand in contrast to those congregations seeking to be contextual is what defines them over against the world in terms of what it means to be Christian in their particular context. The manifest logic used to justify resistance is that maintaining things the way they are is being faithful and obedient to the call and purpose of God. The embedded logic of this approach is that familiarity with *our way of doing things* is preferred and will be protected at all costs. Congregations taking this approach usually end up either becoming ingrown or fighting an endless battle of retrenchment.

Adaptation. A third pattern among some congregations is to seek a strategy of adaptation. The primary approach is to carefully consider cultural and contextual changes in light of the history and traditions of the congregation and the denominational tradition. This framework is then used to make selective adaptive changes in the congregation's ministry that are in line with the heritage while seeking to be responsive to the changed context. This adaptation strategy, unfortunately, tends to be overly internal in focus and usually ends up making too few changes too late to be able to adequately address the changing realities of the context.

The bias of this approach tends to be toward privileging the tradition. While the tradition carries insights into how God's truth was understood and applied in other contexts, the church that is being led by the Spirit recognizes that any tradition must be a living and dynamic reality and that it must take account of new contextual conditions. It is a complex matter to sort out the dynamics of a living tradition in such a way that it can continue to adapt to new circumstances while also being faithful to the values embedded in the tradition.

When we approach the church, however, there is a need to go deeper than any of these responses to changing contexts goes. It is the work of the Spirit that orchestrates the interaction between a congregation and the context in which it is located. The focus of the Spirit's ministry is always to lead the church into redemptive ministry that seeks to transform both human behavior and organizational life as the church participates in God's mission in the world.

The Church as Always *Forming* and *Reforming*

It is necessary to get beyond the limits embedded in the strategies of relevance, resistance, and adaptation. In those strategies, the church either tends to overcontextualize (relevance or adaptation) or undercontextualize (resistance) its identity within a particular context. A fundamentally different approach is required, one that represents the direction of ministry that is inherent to the Spirit-created and Spirit-led missional church. The alternative approach being proposed here is that the church is always both *forming* and *reforming*. This reinforces the logic that the church always needs to be both confessional (claiming and reclaiming its identity in relation to the historic Christian faith) and missional (engaging its context and continuously recontextualizing its ministry). The former inherent impulse was emphasized during the Protestant Reformation around the concept that the *church is always reforming (ecclesia semper reformanda)*. This needs to be complemented by the other inherent impulse which has been developed around the concept of contextualization that the *church is always forming (ecclesia semper formanda)*. When we place these two inherent impulses alongside one another, we have the following:

The church is always forming (missional)—*ecclesia semper formanda*.

The church is always reforming (confessional)—*ecclesia semper reformanda*.

This balancing couplet of ideas is the deeper truth about the church and the ministry of the Spirit that needs to be cultivated. It is a two-pronged truth that draws together the better impulses of the other strategies and places them within a polarity.[4] This polarity creates a dynamic and healthy tension between change and continuity as well as between mission and confession. The leading of the Spirit maintains the tension line between the challenge of recontextualizing a congregation's ministry in the midst of changes taking place in its location and in relation to the challenge of continuing to maintain the truths of the historic Christian faith as these are interpreted and understood by the congregation. The issue is really one of finding the right balance between the two logics of *outside in* and *inside out*. The first one deals with *forming*, while the latter one deals with *reforming*.

On the one hand, congregations are always *forming* even as they are seeking to engage in *reforming*. This means that congregations seek to become contextual even while they seek to maintain the historic Christian faith—an outside-in logic. In doing so, they invite change even while they seek to maintain continuity. The ministry of the Spirit helps congregations engage in both processes simultaneously. This is a polarity, with the actions of one informing the actions of the other. In fact, a congregation's ability to effectively reform will usually be in direct relation to its ability to form a renewed identity in relation to a changing context.

On the other hand, congregations are always *reforming* even as they are continuously *forming*. As noted above, this was one of the great insights of the Protestant Reformation. This insight represents an effort to make congregations more responsive to their heritage by focusing on the inside out. By recovering something from its past through reform, it is hoped that the church will become more responsive to its present. While this can be profoundly true, as demonstrated in the Protestant Reformation, the value of this insight can become misdirected if the focus becomes too inward on what has been and not enough on what now is. There needs to be a balance between the two.

An emerging emphasis today, as noted in chapter 1, is the conversation about the missional church. This represents a change of kind in approaching the issues of change and continuity. The missional church engages in several strategies simultaneously. This reflects its nature as being created by the Spirit. On the one hand, it is always *forming* in relation to new contexts where it seeks to be relevant. It pursues this by reading this context through the lens of the gospel. This opens up new insights of how God is at work and seeking to be at work in that context. On the other hand, the missional church is always *reforming* in relation to the historical Christian faith. It pursues this by rereading the tradition through the lens of the gospel, especially in relation to new insights coming from the interaction of the gospel with a new context.

Understanding the ministry of the Spirit is foundational to understanding the missional church. It is the Spirit who creates the church and gives it a holy nature in the midst of its humanness. This duality is critical to understand, and it is helpful to reflect on it from a number of angles:

Church as seen from above: holy-divine-theological

Church as seen from below: human-historical-sociological

It is this same Spirit who leads the church into ministry in the world as the church lives out of its new nature. While always being shaped within the realities of its humanness, the missional church nevertheless lives by a different set of values and lives out of a different source of empowerment.

The reason the Spirit-led, missional church pursues both of these strategies—always forming and reforming—is because this is part of its very nature. As a community created by the Spirit, the church is missionary by nature. It carries within its DNA both the passion to engage the new while stewarding a proper understanding of the old. This understanding of the church also leads to a different understanding of how the church responds to change. The missional church is always both forming and reforming.

The Spirit-Led, Missional Church in Relationship to Gospel and Culture

The continuous forming and reforming of congregations introduces the dynamics of gospel and culture. This is the territory of the work of the Spirit in the life of congregations. One needs to begin with the Triune God as the creating God to understand fully the ministry of the Spirit in the relationship between gospel and culture. This

God, who created all things, is the same God who seeks to redeem all things (2 Cor. 5:16-21). In fact, God is so passionate about this redemption that God chose to send God's Son into the world to take on human flesh in order to bring about the world's release from its bondage to sin. The gospel is good news for the sake of the world. This means that every context is a location where God seeks to be at work redemptively.

This commitment of God is addressed in one of the great mysteries of the Christian faith, which is that the Word became flesh (John 1:14). God chose to enter the created world and become flesh in the person of Jesus Christ. This act provides us with important insights into understanding the relationship between gospel and culture. The gospel is the good news of God's redemptive intent in the world. We understand the functioning of this intent in light of God's creation design even as we look forward to the final consummation of all things. As the church lives between the times, it understands its existence from three perspectives.

Creation and the missio Dei. God is a creating God who made all that is. God's creation was designed for all of life to flourish. The creation is now fallen in the midst of the presence of sin. But God continues to work within all of creation through the ministry of the Spirit so that all of life may continue to flourish. This is often talked about in theology as the first use of God's law. The law was given so that sin might be restrained, but it was also given so that all of life might flourish. God is passionate about wanting to bring back all things into right relationship. This brings our understanding of the *missio Dei* into relationship with the redemptive reign of God in Christ—what Jesus referred to as the *kingdom of God*. It is in this relationship that the cross meets the creation. This occurs first at the point of the complete fallenness of the world and the gracious offer of the forgiveness of sins, and second at the point of bringing the possibilities of redemptive reconciliation to bear on every dimension of life within the world, so that we might have life abundant.

Re-creation and the kingdom of God. All things were created through Christ in relation to the work of the Spirit; so also, all things can be re-created through Christ in relation to the work of the Spirit. In redemption, the horizon of God's passion is still the world. It is critical that the horizon of the cross be no less. When Jesus announced the presence of the kingdom of God in his person and ministry, he had the whole world in view. The redemptive reign of God in Christ has as its horizon the possibility of bringing back every dimension of life into reconciled relationship with the living God. A proper understanding of the redemptive reign of God in Christ keeps a clear Christology at the center of God's redemptive work within all of creation.

Consummation and the already/not yet. The Spirit of God is moving all things toward God's final consummation and the new heavens and a new earth. The eschatological future of the redemptive power of God has already been released into the world through the work of the Spirit. As such, the church lives between the times. It is already living into the full reality of God's redemptive future—the *already*, even as it awaits the final consummation of the judging of sin and death—the *not yet*. A proper understanding of the already/not yet also keeps a clear eschatology at the center of God's works of creation and re-creation.

Each of these core perspectives of understanding the Spirit-led, missional church involves, of necessity, understanding culture in relation to the work of the Spirit. As discussed in chapter 2, the Spirit was the agent of God to bring the creation into existence, giving birth to both cultures and contexts. The Spirit is also the agent of God to bring the church into existence in the world for the purpose of experiencing salvation and fully living into the redemptive reign of God in Christ. Likewise, the Spirit is the agent of God to engage the reality of every cultural context with the reality of the redemptive reign of God in Christ and the church as God's new creation of community in the world. The amazing thing about this new community is that God's intent and purpose is (a) to bring together persons of diverse cultures and to form them into a new type of community, one that can find unity in the midst of diversity, and (b) to send this community into redemptive ministry within its context. The Spirit leads and teaches this church to engage the world, and in doing so the ministry of the Spirit is carried out in convincing the world of sin, righteousness, and judgment (John 16:8–11). In addressing sin, the Spirit leads the church to unmask the powers that deny life and corrupt human existence. In addressing righteousness, the Spirit leads the church to demonstrate before a watching world the possibilities of what it means to live as redeemed humanity. In addressing

58

judgment, the Spirit holds the world and its rulers accountable as they encounter the church bearing witness to the redemptive reign of God in Christ.

Relating the Work of God's Spirit in the World to Congregations in Particular Contexts

A congregation needs to proactively engage its context. Congregations need to systematically study their contexts to evaluate trends that are taking place. But more importantly, they need to look at their contexts through theological lenses to discern the work of God that is taking place. As noted earlier, change always brings with it new opportunities for ministry as well as challenges that must be addressed. Embedded in a changing context are two key questions that congregations need to regularly ask in relation to the contexts they seek to serve.

What Is God Doing?—The Issue of Faith and Discernment

The first question: What is God doing? This question requires faith and discernment. The world belongs to God. It is God's creation. The church must seek to discern what the Spirit of God is doing in relation to the dynamic changes that are taking place within a particular context. These activities of the Spirit often present fresh opportunities for ministry to congregations. This work of the Spirit in all of creation was presented in chapter 2 and is discussed in more detail in chapter 4 in relation to understanding the ministry of the missional church. For now it is sufficient to note that God is at work in the world beyond the church. Discerning this work of God is foundational for effective ministry. The church is called and sent to participate in God's mission in the world. The responsibility of the church is to discern where and how this mission is unfolding.

The church in Acts—conflict, disruption, interruption, surprise (faith and discernment). Interestingly, the expanded mission and growth of the church under the leading of the Spirit is characterized in the book of Acts as much by conflict, disruption, interruption, and surprise as it is by any planned strategy. This required the church to engage in discernment to interpret what was happening. The point in Acts

59

is clear: The Spirit empowers, teaches, and leads the church, even when the church fails to discern, understand, or engage the fuller purposes of God in living out its missionary nature. Examples of this stand out in the book of Acts, including (a) conflict between groups in the church that led to the recognition of the need to appoint more leadership (Acts 6); (b) a severe persecution that scattered the believers (Acts 8); (c) challenges to the dominant theology that came from the margins of the church at Antioch (Acts 11); (d) a conflict between Barnabas and Paul that led to the emergence of Paul as the primary leader (Acts 15); and (e) the Spirit redirecting the mission team to Macedonia through a vision (Acts 16).

In each of these cases, the church encountered significant change that was neither planned nor anticipated. No strategy was in place that directly led to the growth of the church from these influences. The church was led by the Spirit to move in new directions, which resulted each time in new growth taking place, although not without significant pain and disruption.

What Does God Want to Do?—The Issue of Wisdom and Planning

The second question: What does God want to do? Congregations need to ask on a regular basis in regard to the contexts they seek to serve, What does God want to do? This question requires wisdom and planning. God desires to bring all of life into reconciled relationship. The church must seek to understand how the intent of God, as expressed in the gospel, can work itself out in a particular context to contribute to this ministry of reconciliation. Changes taking place in a ministry context present challenges that the church must seek to address. This requires careful planning. This work of the Spirit is related to the redemptive activity of God in the world. For a church to be a steward of the good news of the gospel, it must engage in focused missional planning in considering how to participate in what God wants to do in a particular context.

The church in Acts—an intentional strategy (wisdom and planning). Within the Spirit's leading of the church in the book of Acts, there are indications that some intentional strategies were used. Being sent necessitates making strategic choices. For example, the Twelve chose to go to the temple daily to proclaim the good news about Jesus, even when forbidden to do so. In a similar manner, Paul and those working with him made a regular practice of trying to win converts in the synagogues from among Jews of the Diaspora as the foundation for planting reproducing churches in key commercial centers of the various provinces of the Roman Empire. As churches were planted, they moved on to the next province, working their way westward.

The church's use of an intentional strategy for evangelizing normally results in expanded mission and the growth of the church, although the church may be redirected at times in how a strategy is actually carried out. For example, Paul and his companions had an intentional plan to get to Ephesus in Asia on Paul's second journey, but were redirected to Macedonia, where they continued with the same strategy of evangelizing persons from synagogues in major cities of key provinces as the basis for starting new congregations.

So then, two patterns are evident in the book of Acts. There is intentional, planned activity that leads to growth—a *strategy* as illustrated in the work of the apostles and Paul's mission team. But there is also the *Spirit's leading* of the church in or through conflict, disruption, interruption, and surprise into new and unanticipated directions that resulted in growth. When considering the ministry of the Spirit-led church, it is essential to utilize wisdom and planning to develop a strategy, but it is also essential to consistently exercise faith and discernment in the midst of unexpected change. A congregation experiences the leading of the Spirit through both processes.

The Gospel as Good News in Every Context

Every congregation is responsible to share the good news about Jesus Christ with others both verbally and through its actions. This responsibility is to be engaged in both corporately and individually by a congregation as it seeks to participate fully in God's mission in the world. But to be good news, the gospel must make sense to those who are hearing it. It must embody the promise that is embedded in the incarnation—that the Word became flesh. In becoming flesh, Jesus Christ as the living Word became understandable, knowable, and accessible for all time and to all persons. The incarnation is a helpful and foundational framework for understanding the inherent translatability of both the gospel and the church.

Inherent Translatability of the Gospel

Jesus as the incarnate Good News took on the particularity of his context. But even in his particularity, he retained his universal relevance.[5] This is part of the mystery of the good news of Jesus Christ. In its particularity we find the promise and the reality of its universality. Just as Jesus, the living Word, took on the particularity of a specific context, so also the gospel of the good news about Jesus Christ is inherently translatable into every particular cultural context with a view toward being universally applicable.[6] This means that it can become good news to *everyone, everywhere*, about *everything* in language and within cultural expressions that are understandable, knowable, and accessible. Through this translatability, this same gospel of good news invites persons to come to know the living and true God and to become enfolded into the worldwide church.

Inherent Translatability of the Church

Just as the gospel is inherently translatable to every cultural context, so also the church is inherently translatable in the same way. The church that is professed as being catholic, as stated in the Apostles' Creed and the Nicene Creed, is able to find expression *everywhere*. This same church, then, has the inherent ability to live *every place*, to become contextual within any and every setting. The church that is missionary by nature inherently seeks its contextuality—it seeks to become responsive within and adaptive to every context in which it finds itself.[7]

These premises regarding the inherent translatability of the gospel and the church have profound implications for mission and evangelizing. The church is responsible to translate the good news of the gospel along with its own organizational reality into every cultural context that it encounters. To do so requires that the church plan strategically for this work even as it seeks to discern the leading of the Spirit. As noted in the book of Acts, this often comes through conflict, disruption, interruption, and surprise as much as it does through planning and strategy. Through strategy as well as through discernment, the church must engage the principalities and powers of every context with the redemptive power of God. This leads to the importance of understanding the inherent aptitudes of the Spirit-led, missional church.

Aptitudes of Spirit-Led, Missional Congregations in Context

The Spirit of God not only creates the church by calling it into existence, the Spirit of God also leads the church by sending it into the world to participate fully in God's mission in all of creation. This means that congregations are missionary by nature. This Spirit-created missionary nature provides congregations with certain inherent aptitudes that need to be cultivated so that Spirit-led ministry can be expressed. The following seven aptitudes represent dimensions of how the Spirit-created church is to live out Spirit-led ministry.

Aptitude 1—Spirit-led, missional congregations learn to read a context as they seek their contextuality. It is critical that congregations develop the ability to read a context. This is an aptitude that is inherent within the church being missionary by nature. This means that a church that is Spirit-led will always seek to be contextual wherever it is located. To do so faithfully and effectively, the church must understand its context. The importance of this aptitude has become increasingly recognized in recent years, and many tools have been developed to assist congregations in this task.[8] The key point, however, is that the *reading of the context* should not be limited to its demographics and sociology. It should also include a theological reading of this data. This is where the faith-and-discernment task of answering the question, What is God doing? comes into play. This analysis of the context also brings the other responsibility into focus, that of wisdom and planning, which asks the question, What does God want to do?

Aptitude 2—Spirit-led, missional congregations anticipate new insights into the gospel. As the gospel engages new cultures within various contexts, Spirit-led, missional congregations anticipate new insights into understanding the fuller meaning of the gospel. The act of translating the Bible into new vernacular languages often opens up fresh understandings regarding the meaning of the gospel. This is illustrated in the New Testament when the gospel was translated into a Hellenistic worldview at Antioch. The Hellenized version of understanding the gospel helped break Jewish Christianity out of its provincialism and later became the normative expression of the faith for centuries to come.[9]

Lamin Sanneh makes this same point regarding the translation of the gospel into the African context. In spite of all the transplanted Western forms, the gospel found its indigenous voice within the cultures of the African peoples as new expressions of the faith and new forms of churches emerged.[10] This aptitude of missional congregations anticipating new insights into the gospel is related to these same congregations always *forming* within their context. In doing so, fresh resources for understanding the faith are often released.

Aptitude 3: Spirit-led, missional congregations anticipate reciprocity. One of the interesting things about the ministry of the Spirit is that over time the gospel often brings about reciprocity. Reciprocity occurs when the cultural group that brings the gospel into a different context is itself changed over time by those who received the gospel. An example of this in the book of Acts is Peter's encounter with Cornelius (Acts 10). This story is as much about the continuing conversion of Peter as it is about the conversion of Cornelius. Another example is the spillover effect of the persecution described in Acts 8 that resulted, seemingly circumstantially, in the development of the Gentile church in Antioch (Acts 11). Given time, the gospel that was proclaimed at Antioch as "salvation by grace through faith plus nothing" came to be accepted as the gospel of the entire church (Acts 15).

In the latter example, what began on the margins came to the center. This is often the case with reciprocity. An example of this in the U.S. today is evident through many of the newer immigrant communities. Coming from churches in what were former foreign mission fields, many new immigrant congregations are now relocating within established Anglo communities, both urban and rural. These congregations are inviting a deeper level of understanding the gospel's call for reconciled unity between Christians. Many are also bringing their own missionary activity into the U.S., where they view their new location as being in need of hearing the gospel, once again, for the first time.

Aptitude 4: Spirit-led, missional congregations understand they are contextual and, therefore, are also particular. Our language illustrates this point whenever we refer to a congregation as a local church. "Local" means that, of necessity, a congregation is particular to its time and place. While it is also catholic, bearing the full marks of the church universal and the historic Christian faith, it is profoundly local in contextualizing these realities to the community it seeks to serve.

This local-catholic dynamic means that there is always a certain provisional character about the church as it lives within a context. As contexts change, the church should expect to change, even as it attempts to live out the tension inherent in being faithful to the gospel while also being responsive to the context. This point introduces the important issue of how *models* function in relation to congregations. In reality, there can be *no model congregation*. While there can be illustrative examples of contextualized congregations that might help inform others, no congregation can function as a model for others to replicate. It is important to remember that it is the work of the Spirit to lead a congregation to contextualize itself within its particular location.

Aptitude 5: Spirit-led, missional congregations understand that ministry is always contextual and, therefore, is also practical. Missional congregations understand that the practice of ministry is always normed by Scripture, but they also understand that this takes place in the particular contexts that they serve. Just as a congregation is always contextual, so also its ministry is always contextual. The Spirit leads congregations within particular contexts. Ministry can only take place in relation to a particular context, and as ministry takes place specific practices are developed for that context.

This particularity of ministry means that all forms of Spirit-led ministry are going to reflect the patterns and shape of the culture in which a congregation is ministering. The necessary practices that are developed are the practical outworking of this ministry. This introduces the important issue of how *programs* function in relation to congregations. In reality, there can be *no common program* that works the same in each congregation and context. While a basic programmatic framework might inform the development of ministry, each congregation is best served by thinking carefully about how such a program needs to be adapted to best fit its particular ministry and the context being served.

Aptitude 6: Spirit-led, missional congregations understand that doing theology is always contextual and, therefore, is also perspectival. Congregations articulate their confessed faith in what is generally referred to as "theology." This understanding is shaped by historical, confessional perspectives, but Spirit-led, missional congregations understand that these perspectives have embedded within them elements of the culture and context in which they were formulated. While theological expressions bear witness to the larger reality of God's truth, they must always be understood as reflecting a particular time and place. The theological expressions of a particular time and place can still have relevance for many other contexts, but there is always a need to engage in interpreting and translating them when moving from one context to another.

This introduces the important issue of how *confessions* function in relation to congregational life. In reality there can be *no universal confession*. Every congregation needs to learn how to *confess the faith* within its particular context. While congregations need to draw on historical confessions to engage in confessing the faith, they need to actively engage in translating the themes and insights of historical confessions in order to address the issues within their own contexts.

Aptitude 7: Spirit-led, missional congregations understand that organization is always contextual and, therefore, is also provisional. A Spirit-led, missional congregation develops organizational forms to carry out its ministry and to structure its life. It must be understood that these forms bear the imprint of particular contexts. Organization in congregations is, therefore, always contextual and provisional in character. While there are biblical principles that function across a wide range of contexts, the particular forms that emerge must be seen as being particular to specific contexts. This is part of the good news of the gospel, that congregations are able to relate to any culture and to any context.

The challenge is to allow the leading of the Spirit to give birth to forms that are informed by the historic Christian faith, while also reflecting the realities of the context in which congregations are located. This introduces the important issue of how *polity* is to function in relation to congregations. In reality, there can be *no standardized polity*. Polity needs to focus more on guiding principles rather than prescribed practices. This is because polities need to be adaptive and flexible in consciously taking context and culture into consideration in the midst of the ongoing processes of *forming* and *reforming*.

Summary

The leading of the Spirit always takes place in relation to specific contexts. This means that the leading of the Spirit involves the church learning to be in ministry within a specific context. It is important to understand how the church came to be contextualized within the specific context of the U.S. It is also important to explore the issue of how the church can sometimes become overly contextualized. The next chapter examines these issues and contrasts them with an understanding of the Spirit-led, missional church.

CHAPTER 4

Spirit-Led Ministry in the U.S. Context and in the Missional Church

A conversation emerged among several pastors from diverse denominations at the monthly luncheon for area pastors about how authority is best exercised in the church. Pastor David, a Baptist, wanted to know how anyone could submit to the authority of a bishop. Pastor Lydia, an Episcopalian, responded by inquiring how congregations could ever hope to have any sense of shared identity without some type of central authority. Pastor Carol, a Presbyterian, noted that she agreed with the importance of having central authority but that this functioned best when lodged within a representative body rather than one person. Pastor John, a United Methodist, observed that authority seemed to function best when there was a central person with authority that functioned in relation to a representative body.

As the conversation unfolded, Pastor Bill, an ELCA Lutheran, finally observed that views on authority seemed to be as diverse as the number of denominations that were represented. He went on to inquire, "How did we get to this point, where we have so many different denominations?"

Most Christian congregations in the U.S. reflect in their identity, either directly or indirectly, something of the unique circumstances surrounding the emergence of the church during the colonial period and the uniting of the states into a national government.[1] This follows the point developed in chapter 3 that the church under the leading of the Spirit seeks to become contextual and therefore takes on characteristics of its cultural context. However, one of the challenges facing the church is that it can become overly contextualized within a particular cultural context. This is one of the reasons why the church is always in need of *reforming*, even while it engages in *forming* new practices in relation to continued changes in its context. As the church in the U.S. has formed and reformed over the past several centuries, a wide variety of organizational expressions have come into existence. All of these need to be understood as being part of the visible church in this context.

The Variety of Organizational Expressions of the Visible Church in the U.S.

The visible church is that church which can be found within the world at any point in time, and which consists of all the rich diversity of people and organizational expressions of the church that exist. What is important to note is that the catholicity of the church assumes its contextuality. In other words, if the church is able to exist everywhere, then it must be able to become contextual in every place. The inherent diversity of organizational expressions within the contextualized catholicity of the church is not only to be expected, it is also to be valued. This is an affirmation that in the midst of being many, the church is also one.[2] So also, the inherent unity within this diversity is also to be expected and valued. Unfortunately, the church seems to find that expressing its diversity is an easier purpose to pursue than cultivating its essential unity. In order to gain some perspective on the complexity of this challenge, it is helpful to map the various organizational expressions that can be found in the visible church in the U.S.

Congregations. The most common expressions of the church in the world are the gathered communities of faith that we have come to know as congregations. They come in all shapes and sizes and express an incredibly wide range of both theological understandings and organizational forms.

Regional judicatories. Most congregations are organized as a part of something larger than themselves. Typically, they relate to other congregations of their denomination within a geographic area in some type of official church body such as a presbytery, synod, diocese, conference, or association.

Larger assemblies and denominations. Most regional judicatories are part of a larger organizational structure. Typically, these are built around some type of theological tradition and historical polity—e.g., Reformed, Lutheran, Charismatic, Baptist, Mennonite, Catholic, or Orthodox.

Boards and agencies. Every denomination of any size has created some internal organizational structures, usually agencies under board governance, to carry out various ministries. Most denominations continue to struggle with integrating the role and authority of such internal agencies and boards with the authority of the larger assemblies.

Parachurch organizations. Outside the formal structures of denominations are found a wide range of parachurch organizations. Most of these have a specialized focus in terms of their purpose and ministry, as is evident in organizations such as Young Life, Campus Crusade for Christ, Wycliffe Bible Translators, and Youth with a Mission.

Emerging associations and networks. Still other regional or associational connections function as networks, where congregations participate primarily in terms of sharing information or resources. A good example of this today is the Willow Creek Association with its over eleven thousand member congregations.[3]

Movements and Conversations. Yet one more organizational expression of the visible church is what might be best defined as a movement or a conversation. A movement or conversation takes on a shared life among large numbers of persons in terms of purpose and support but without necessarily any formal commitments being made. Examples of some movements include Right to Life, Promise Keepers, and study courses offered through Alpha; an example of a conversation is the emerging church.

These diverse expressions of the visible church in the U.S. context represent various historical developments that have taken place. When considering the contextual character of congregations in the U.S., it is helpful to have some perspective regarding how these various organizational structures came into existence. The focus in what follows will pay primary attention to the emergence of the denominational, corporate church with its numerous congregations, but the forces which shaped this type of church also helped to give birth to the other organizational expressions noted above. And all of these organizational expressions share a similar genetic code.

It was in the milieu of the colonial setting and the formation of the United States that the modern expression of the *denominational* church emerged. This represented a substantially new understanding of the church at that time, one that to this day continues to dramatically shape our understanding of congregations. While congregations can be classified through a wide array of types,[4] what is interesting about the vast majority of Christian congregations in the U.S. is one characteristic they tend to share in common. At the core of their identity, what might be labeled as a part of their genetic code, is an organizational self-understanding related to a purposive intent.[5] This tends to lead to a functional or instrumental view of the church where a congregation's primary identity is related to it being responsible to accomplish something. This functional ecclesiology (instrumental view of the church) of an organizational self-understanding (church viewed primarily from an organizational perspective) related to a purposive intent (church understood as needing to do something) is at the heart of the identity of what is being referred to here as the *corporate church*.

This understanding of the church is quite different from two other ways in which the church can be conceived. One is the *established church* where the church's self-understanding is that it serves as the primary location of God's presence and activity in the world. This conception of church came into existence in the fourth century with the establishment of Constantinian Christendom and continues to this day within many Catholic countries and in a variety of Protestant state churches.[6] The other is the *missional church* where the church's self-understanding is that it is a social community created by the Spirit that is called and sent to participate fully in God's mission in the world. These three self-understandings provide the framework for thinking further about the responsibility of congregations to be Spirit-led as they become contextual. First, the differences between the established church and the corporate church will be developed, along with an overview of the historical development of the corporate church. This will be followed by a discussion of the differences between the corporate church and the missional church. The chart below sets up these two points of comparison, and what follows will explain these different understandings of the church.

Established Church	Corporate Church	Missional Church
Self-understanding: Exists as the primary geographical location of God's presence on earth through which the world can encounter God, with this authority being legitimated by the civil government.	Self-understanding: Exists as an organization with a purposive intent to accomplish something on behalf of God in the world, with this role being legitimated on a voluntary basis.	Self-understanding: Exists as a community created by the Spirit that is missionary by nature in being called and sent to participate in God's mission in the world.

Established Church versus Corporate Church

The self-understanding of the corporate church is quite different from the self-understanding of the established church that emerged within Europe in relation to Constantinian Christendom. Congregations within established churches, whether Roman Catholic or Protestant, carry a self-understanding of being the institutional expression of the geographical location of God's presence on earth as the one, true church. While they have an organizational makeup, the key to their legitimacy within their self-understanding is that their existence represents the primary horizon of God's activity in the world.[7] The problems associated with this understanding became painfully evident in the wars of religion that raged throughout Europe from the late 1500s into the early 1600s. The eventual "solution" that was rendered—*whose realm, whose religion*—ended those hostilities but left unresolved the core self-understanding of the established church.[8] This is reflected in the continued efforts most established churches made in persecuting other expressions of the church—what they labeled as *sects*. Such "sects" were understood to be illegitimate.[9]

Interestingly, immigrants from the European state churches as well as immigrants from among many of the sects persecuted by them began to settle after 1600 in the colonies of what eventually became the United States. Here they found that a different core identity was required to give legitimacy to the church. This alternative conception came into existence around an organizational self-understanding related to a purposive intent, what is being referred to here as the *corporate church*. By the mid-to-late 1700s, this view became the normative understanding of the newly forming denominations and their congregations in the colonies. Since then, the corporate church has gone through several phases of development over the past two hundred plus years, but the basic genetic code of its self-understanding remains at the center of its identity.

Formation of the Corporate Church

The introduction above provides a basic framework for understanding the difference between the established church, the corporate church, and the missional church. However, to gain a deeper understanding of these differences, it is useful to review the historical development of the formation of the corporate church. The basic premise is that the corporate church finds its primary identity within an organizational self-understanding in relation to a purposive intent. As also noted above, this understanding leads us to think about the church primarily, though not necessarily exclusively, in *functional* terms where the church is responsible to do something. This is often expressed as being out of obedience to accomplish something on behalf of God in the world (e.g., being obedient to carry out the Great Commission). It is important to note that the formation and development of the corporate church has been dynamic over time. The five phases of the formation of the corporate church within denominational church life in the U.S. are summarized below.[10]

The Colonial Experience, 1600s–1780s

The formation of the American colonies was the result of diverse interests. Some were economic, some were political, some were social, but embedded in the colonial experience some motives were also deeply religious. Many of the more radical sectarian groups in Europe immigrated to the colonies to secure their religious freedom. Some of these groups, such as the Puritans in the New England colonies, attempted to set up their own version of what might be identified as a type of state church, which some, as Sydney E. Ahlstrom notes,

74

have inappropriately labeled as a theocracy.[11] But dissenting groups within these colonies soon challenged this approach, such as the Baptists in Rhode Island. While the Congregationalists (former Puritans) created an established church in the New England colonies, the seeds of religious diversity in these areas were planted and began taking root by the early 1700s.[12]

Joining the various immigrant groups of sectarian dissenters were numerous immigrants from the state churches of Europe, especially of English Anglicans but also the Scottish Presbyterians, the Dutch Reformed, and the German and Scandinavian Lutherans. In addition, Roman Catholic immigrants also settled into some areas, especially the colony of Maryland. Although the Anglicans established a territorial, parish-church system in most of the southern colonies, by the early 1700s these areas were also experiencing the reality of religious diversity.[13]

This shared experience of religious diversity throughout the colonies required a new imagination for how to conceive of the church and how to organize congregations. The established identity of a state church that allowed it the privilege of persecuting other Christian sects was obsolete almost from the beginning. However, it took time for this view to be fully deconstructed, and vestiges of it even lingered into the early 1800s in several New England states after the decision to separate the church and the state.[14] A new identity was required in the face of the rise of religious diversity, a diversity that was most prevalent in the middle colonies (New Jersey, Maryland, Pennsylvania, and Delaware). It was in these colonies that a new identity was first formulated.[15]

The formation of this new identity, what is here being identified as the *corporate church with an organizational self-understanding related to a purposive intent*, resulted primarily from the coalescence of two movements. One movement was the development of free-church ecclesiology as the norm for understanding the church within the colonies. This ecclesiology had emerged over against the European state churches from among the Anabaptists. The Anabaptists conceived of the church primarily in terms of being a gathered social community of persons who possessed the freedom to associate and the right to govern their own affairs.[16] While many churches in the colonies brought with them the ecclesiologies and polities of their European state churches, the new context of religious diversity required adjustments almost from the beginning.[17] The primary adjustment made by all toward the end of the 1700s, given the colonial separation of church and state, was the adoption of some form of a free-church ecclesiology. This was done either as the formal ecclesiology or at least as an overlay on the previous established, state-church ecclesiology.

A second movement that contributed to the formation of the corporate church also emerged in the context of the colonial experience. The recently arrived European immigrants had to construct a new social order. While many patterns of European society were carried by the immigrants into the colonies, new social constructions were also required. One important feature of the new society in the colonies was the *voluntary association*.[18] By the early 1800s, Alexis de Tocqueville would identify this characteristic as one of the more unique features of the emerging American society.[19] The rich fabric of voluntary associations within the colonies included many that were secular in origin and others that were religious. Some of the religious voluntary organizations were shared between various church bodies, while others served the needs of particular churches. This set of organizational structures reflected the democratic principles that were being nurtured in the colonies as well as the natural extension of the logic of free-church ecclesiology. These structures deeply impacted the genetic code of the corporate church that was emerging.[20]

The outlines of the corporate church were coming clearly into focus by the mid-1700s. The call for independence and the Revolutionary War cemented its formation. In the First Amendment of the Bill of Rights, which was proposed in 1789, a provision was made for the legal separation of church and state.[21] No church would be established. Every church would be protected to practice religious freedom. The organizing principle of denominationalism was affirmed with this decision, which gave impetus to the further development of the corporate church. Within the last two decades of the 1700s, representatives of numerous church bodies in the newly formed United States met to form national organizations.[22] This brings us to the next phase of the development of the corporate church.

The Purposive Denomination, 1790–1870

The newly formed denominations were unique. As noted by church historian Martin Marty, they represented a unique turning point in the history of the church, one which departed from the previous 1,400 years of the church's self-understanding as an established church.[23] The denominational, organizational church—the early version of the corporate church—was a unique creation within the American setting. Largely, the denominational, organizational church was the pragmatic result of a variety of circumstances and events. Interestingly, although some historical precedents were available, these developments were usually rationalized biblically and theologically after the fact, if at all.[24] By 1800, most of the newly formed denominations had created assembly structures at three levels—a national assembly, regional judicatories, and local congregations.

The use of the word *denomination* to describe initially the churches in the colonies and later in the U.S. came from the term given to alternative forms of church with the adoption of the Act of Toleration in England in 1689.[25] The inherent logic of a denomination is that it is organized to do something, normally with a focus on doing something on behalf of God in the world. It has an organizational self-understanding related to a purposive intent which means it must do something in order to justify its existence. It is essentially functional, or instrumental in its identity and purpose. This follows the logic of organizational sociology where organizations, once formed, seek to accomplish some goal.[26] While this meaning of organization was also true of the established church, it was not the primary characteristic of the self-understanding of that church. The corporate church represents a significant shift away from the identity of the established church that understood itself as the primary location of God's presence and activity in the world. Building on the foundations of free-church ecclesiology, denominations and their congregations were formed around a functional and organizational rationale for their existence.

A significant challenge faced the newly forming denominations in the late 1700s and early 1800s as the frontier opened up beyond the Allegheny Mountains. In response, the various denominations geared up to bring the church to this expanding frontier as settlers poured through the passes into the hinterland. This challenge represented a worthy goal that needed to be addressed.

Inspired largely in the early 1800s by the revivals of the Second Great Awakening on the frontier, the congregations of different denominations developed a variety of methods to carry out their functional purpose of bringing the church to these new regions. Methodologies such as camp meetings, anxious benches, itinerant preachers, and Sunday schools became the order of the day.[27] Conflicts over the use of such *measures* were not uncommon, and even led to a split between the Old School and New School Presbyterians in 1837.[28] This expanding work on the frontier required new organizational structures at the national level of these denominations. Paralleling this work was the rapidly growing interest in what became know as *foreign missions*.[29] By the 1830s, what had earlier been committees or boards that were made up of active pastors and lay leaders became formal, denominational agencies at the national level, which had permanent staff.[30] The purpose of such agencies was to plan for and to coordinate the expanding ministries of domestic and foreign missions, along with such emerging ministries of Christian education and publishing houses.

These newly formed denominational agencies, with their representative boards, reflected the logic of what had been either a mission society in Europe (see William Carey[31]) or the mutually shared, Christian voluntary organizations in the U.S.[32] Such extrachurch structures have today come to be known as parachurch organizations. Once again, they were largely the creation of organizational structure out of pragmatic necessity rather than being the result of careful reflection on ecclesiology and polity. They were not without controversy in some denominations,[33] but most every denomination followed this pattern during the early 1800s. The biggest question left unresolved in their formation was the relationship between the formal denominational agencies to the previously formed assembly structures of the new national denominations.

The initial logic of the corporate church had vested its self-understanding within its representative assemblies at the national, regional, and local levels. Now a new organizational dimension was placed into the mix—the denominational agency with its representative board. Which would lead? Which was to be subordinate? It soon became clear that the assembly structures would maintain primary control. This was largely the result of the translated polities from European state churches that had built vertically structured organizational assemblies within their contexts of having domain. In such contexts, they did not have the need to develop the horizontal missionary structures that became common in the U.S. A clear example of this can be seen in the development of mission structures by the Presbyterian Church in the early 1800s, when first a board was added and later an agency to engage in mission work. A substantial theological argument was offered for making boards and their agencies subservient to the assemblies, but this argument largely assumed the backdrop of the state church pattern of assembly.[34]

By the mid-to-late 1800s, the modern organizational, denominational church had become the norm for church life in the U.S. Congregations of a particular denomination usually differentiated their existence from others primarily in terms of theological and confessional distinctives. These distinctives were also related to the different polities of the Congregational (autonomy of the local church to govern its life), Presbyterian (representative governing body beyond the congregations), and Episcopal (government by bishops) forms of church government. But underneath these theological, confessional, and polity differences lay a common genetic code. The corporate church was now the common reality for most denominations—at the national, regional, and local levels and within their boards and agencies.

The Churchly Denomination, 1870–1920

Coming out of the Civil War, most denominations began to develop a more elaborate infrastructure as the frontier rapidly filled in and as cities began to grow. By the latter part of the 1800s, another phase in the development of the corporate church became discernible. Refined methodologies for developing new congregations were developed as existing congregations came to be supported in new ways.[35]

During this time, most churches began to take on a more programmatic approach to their ministries. In education, standardized curriculums for the expanding Sunday school systems were formed and put into place by denominational publishing houses.[36] Denominational youth ministries came into existence by the late 1800s, often patterned after the parachurch ministry of Christian Endeavor.[37] By the turn of the century, especially in the new urban congregations, one began to see such programmatic activities as the construction of extensive educational buildings that accommodated classes for instruction broken down by age and gender, the formation of robed choirs, the provision of a variety of recreational facilities for family activities, and the development of church libraries. In effect, a total church program was being put into place that would deal with members from cradle to grave.[38]

Also during this period an increasing number of ministers were becoming seminary trained, leading to a growing professionalization of the clergy. Related to this development was the increased importance of seminaries within denominational church life. In the midst of these changes, denominations were becoming complex, organizational systems with multiple boards and agencies at the national level. Over time, these national-level structures began to find their counterparts at the regional level, and even to some extent at the local level, where organized committees tended to parallel the design of the national church. The churchly denomination was now a reality and new approaches to governing them were being required.[39]

The Corporate Denomination, 1920–1970

While the suggested date that divides the previous phase from this current phase is somewhat arbitrary, a discernible shift became evident within denominational church life during the first decades of the twentieth century. As noted above, the growing complexity of the churchly denomination required new ways for structuring and managing the church. Interestingly, during this period of time the newly emerging field of organizational management was gaining influence. Although several sources were involved in the formation of this new social science discipline, the most important for denominations in the U.S. was the stream stemming from Frederick Taylor and what became known as Scientific Management.[40] This movement focused on bringing productivity and efficiency into the business organization. It did so by de-skilling tasks, organizing similar work activities into functional units, and building coordination systems through the establishment of hierarchical bureaucracy.

This movement found a voice in the emerging world of complex, churchly denominations through the work of Shailer Mathews, dean of the Chicago School of Divinity, who in 1912 published *Scientific*

Management in the Churches. The focus was on treating the church as "something of a business establishment."[41] The increasingly rationalized world of the modern bureaucracy began to become the norm for denominational church life. Boards and agencies at the national level increasingly adopted corporate forms of organization and management as the number of departments was expanded and more staff were increasingly added.

By the end of World War II, when the rapidly growing suburbanization of the church took place, the corporate denomination was well positioned to wage the campaign of starting new corporate congregations in cooperation with their corporate judicatories. High birth rates for over two decades (the baby-boom generation from 1946–1964), an expanding middle class, increasing levels of education, the mass-produced automobile, three-dollar-a-barrel oil, a newly expanding interstate highway system, and the creation of the thirty-year fixed-rate mortgage all contributed to making the suburbs become the new destination of choice.[42] Migration from both the central cities and rural areas fed the growth of these suburbs. Continued high levels of denominational loyalty during this period allowed for the rapid growth of suburban congregations among almost all denominations.

Thousands of organizational, denominational congregations were started. The logic of the corporate church was now coming to full expression as the good life of the American dream was packaged and commodified as the suburban ideal.[43] It was an ideal to which millions aspired but which was mostly realized by the emerging white middle class. The darker side of this suburban success was what Gibson Winter labeled in 1962 as the "suburban captivity."[44] With its profound success during the two and half decades from 1945–1970, the denominational, organizational, suburban congregation extended the logic of the organizational self-understanding of the corporate church to a new level.

The primary logic of the previous city-neighborhood congregation had continued to be a mixture of intergenerational relationships that operated in the midst of an increasing programmatic structure that was fed by the denominational agencies. But in the suburban congregation people's relationships became largely functional, becoming tied to attendance at a variety of activities rather than being rooted primarily in a shared sense of social community. This shift was partially the result of the increased rates of mobility in society and the difficulty of developing sustained relationships. Here a corporate identity came to be established primarily around shared programmatic activities.[45] It is interesting that the small group movement began to emerge during this time to try to bring some sense of social community back into congregational life. The organizational, program phase of the corporate church was now in full bloom. What is also interesting is how rapidly this type of congregational understanding of the corporate church imploded in the midst of the dramatic cultural shifts of the 1960s and 1970s.

A whole range of movements define this transitional period—e.g., the civil rights movement, the youth movement/counterculture, the feminist movement, the ecological movement, and the anti-war movement, among others. But what is important to note is the rapid collapse of institutional identity among the emerging generation.[46] The boomer generation left the church in greater numbers than any previous generation and came back in fewer numbers. The starting of new congregations by denominations as franchise models came to a screeching halt by the mid-1970s.[47] Standardized, denominational educational curriculums went into decline and most were out of business by the 1980s. In the midst of these dramatic changes, the corporate church entered into yet another phase of development.

The Regulatory Denomination and Emerging New Networks, 1970 to Date

There have been two primary shifts taking place since the 1970s. On the one hand, the more traditional denominations, especially mainline denominations, have struggled to maintain their viability.[48] On the other hand, a whole new pattern of emerging networks have begun to come into existence, which portray many of the patterns of denominations but which are also quite different in other ways.[49]

Traditional denominations. Many traditional denominations, especially those known as the mainline, are now in substantial decline. While some of the more conservative or evangelical denominations are still growing, many of the forces of change impacting the mainline are also affecting their ministries. Revenue to national church offices is dramatically down, which in turn has led to continued downsizing of national agencies and churchwide staff.[50] The median age of members of most mainline denominations now exceeds the national median age in many cases by twenty or more years (fifty-five and older versus thirty-five).[51] In the midst of these changes in the mainline denominations, some of those that are more conservative have shown growth, and a new movement of independent congregations is now rapidly expanding.[52]

Clearly, we are currently in a period of transition in the life of the corporate church in the U.S. From the 1960s through the 1990s, new movements emerged that tried to give direction in the midst of the changes that were taking place, all of them working primarily from a functional ecclesiology of an instrumental view of the church. The church renewal movement of the 1960s and early 1970s focused on trying to make existing structures more relevant to a new generation in the midst of a rapidly changing context. The church growth movement of the 1970s and early 1980s placed emphasis on evangelism and focused largely on pragmatic technique. By the 1980s and early 1990s, the church effectiveness/health movement brought the wider range of a social science, organizational perspective to bear on trying to manage and lead congregations through renewal and growth in the midst of change.[53]

In the midst of these movements, a host of market-driven models of church, or what some have labeled as "mission-driven," came into existence.[54] The seeker-church phenomenon pioneered by Willow Creek Community Church is probably the most influential, especially as it came to be operationalized into the *purpose-driven church* by Saddleback Church under the leadership of Rick Warren.[55] At the heart of these various market-driven or mission-driven models is a theology of the Great Commission where mission is understood primarily as something the church must do, which reinforces a functional view of the corporate church within its organizational self-understanding related to a purposive intent.

Declining denominations have not been immune to these recent movements as they struggle to reinvent the logic of the corporate church. Many have created internal versions of similar programmatic approaches. But overall, the corporate church within denominational church life has tended to become more regulatory in character. When denominational loyalty is lost, one of the options available is to turn to rules and procedures to seek compliance. Another option available is to try to reinvent the core identity. But the genetic code of the corporate church has yet to be sufficiently examined to allow for this. Those who have gone this route tend to still work inside of the same assumptions of a functional approach to ecclesiology and polity, a view that gave birth to the corporate church to begin with.[56]

Emerging new networks. There is clearly a new pattern in how many congregations now express their understanding and practice of the catholicity of the church, i.e., of being a part of the larger whole. A whole series of associations and networks have emerged in recent decades, usually around shared interest. These have become most apparent in relation to the rapid growth of what are referred to as the megachurches (e.g., Willow Creek Association[57]), along with the recent development of the emerging church (e.g., Emergent Village[58]). We now find new patterns of associating and networking among congregations that cut across denominational lines and represent a wide range of interests, such as mission (e.g., the Lausanne Committee on World Evangelization or the Frontier Mission movement), worship renewal (e.g., Charismatic Renewal or Concerts of Prayer), discipleship and evangelism (e.g., The Alpha Course or Bible Study Fellowship), and single-purpose moral agendas (e.g., Right to Life).

The Corporate Church versus Missional Church

The contrast between the established church and the corporate church is critical to understand in dealing with congregations in the U.S. Likewise, the contrast between the corporate church and the missional church is also becoming critical to understand because the issues of ecclesiology and polity from a missional perspective are now front and center. The table below sets up this contrast.

Established Church	Corporate Church	Missional Church
Self-understanding: Exists as the primary geographical location of God's presence on earth through which the world can encounter God, with this authority being legitimated by the civil government.	Self-understanding: Exists as an organization with a purposive intent to accomplish something on behalf of God in the world, with this role being legitimated on a voluntary basis.	Self-understanding: Exists as a community created by the Spirit that is missionary by nature in being called and sent to participate in God's mission in the world.

A vibrant discussion took place during the last half of the twentieth century regarding ecclesiology, i.e., the doctrine of the church. Expressions of this discussion were evident in such developments as the formation of the World Council of Churches (WCC) in 1947 from the earlier Faith and Order and Life and Work movements, the merger of the former International Missionary Council (IMC) into the WCC in 1961, Vatican II in the early 1960s, multiple church mergers in the U.S. throughout the 1960s, and a convergence in missiological circles around a mission theology related to the *missio Dei* and the kingdom of God. By the end of the twentieth century, these various movements and discussions led to a fresh understanding of ecclesiology from a missiological perspective, what has come to be known as the *missional church*.[59]

The missional church conversation brings together two streams of understanding God's work in the world. First, God has a mission within all of creation—the *missio Dei*. Second, God brought redemption to bear on all of life within creation through the life, death, and resurrection of Jesus Christ—the kingdom of God. This redemptive work of God through Christ is best understood in terms of its announcement and inauguration by Jesus as the presence of the kingdom of God in the world.

A missional understanding of God's work in the world from this perspective is framed as follows: God is seeking to bring his kingdom, the redemptive reign of God in Christ, to bear on every dimension of life within all the world so that the larger creation purposes of God can be fulfilled—the *missio Dei*. This missional understanding has the world as its primary horizon and the church is placed at the center of the activity in relating the kingdom of God to the *missio Dei*. The church's self-understanding of being missional is grounded in the work of the Spirit of God, who calls the church into existence as a gathered community, equips and prepares it, and sends it into the world to participate fully in God's mission.

Interestingly, the missional church conversation has introduced a new dimension into the discussion of the identity of the church. At the center of this conversation is the relationship of the church to its context in light of a different understanding of the nature or essence of the church. In this conversation, mission is no longer understood primarily in functional terms as something the church *does*, as is the

85

case for the corporate church. Rather it is understood in terms of something the church *is*, as something that is related to its nature. But also of importance in this conversation, mission is not subsumed under ecclesiology, as is true for the established church where the church is seen as the primary location of God's activity in the world. The missional church, in contrast, shifts the focus to the world as the horizon for understanding the work of God and the identity of the church. This understanding is expressed in terms of the relationship of the *missio Dei* (the larger mission of God) to the *kingdom of God* (the redemptive reign of God in Christ). The *organizational self-understanding related to a purposive intent* of the corporate church is replaced by a *missional self-understanding* of the church. To catch the fuller implications of this shift of perspective one needs to understand the biblical and theological foundations for the missional church—what might be called a missiological ecclesiology.[60]

Trinitarian Foundations for Ecclesiology

There have been significant developments in the past few decades in trinitarian studies regarding an understanding of mission. It should be noted that the emergence of the concept of mission has its roots in the colonial period of Catholic missions.[61] The twentieth century saw the unraveling of the massive colonial systems spawned by both Roman Catholic and Protestant nations over the previous several centuries. In their embarrassment, many churches in the West that had come to be associated with these colonial systems began dropping such words as *mission* or *missions* out of their ecclesiastical vocabulary during the last half of the twentieth century.[62] However, during this same period some significant developments took place in trinitarian studies that began to bring missiology into direct conversation with ecclesiology.

Growing out of the strong tradition of biblical theology that emerged in the 1930s and 1940s, several important theological streams began to find their voice shortly after midcentury. One stream is represented in the work done by the former International Missionary Council (IMC). Building on a renewed emphasis on the role of the kingdom of God in relation to mission as expressed during the Whitby gathering in 1947, the Willengen meeting of the IMC in

1952 gave fresh expression to understanding mission. Although not formally used until after the conference when the summary documents were prepared, the concept of *missio Dei* was formulated in trinitarian terms as the foundation for engaging in mission.[63] The emphasis was placed on the mission of the Triune God in the world in relation to all three persons of the Godhead—Father, Son, and Holy Spirit. Subsequent meetings of the IMC and its successor body, the Commission on World Mission and Evangelism (CWME) within the WCC, continued to draw on this significant reconceptualization of mission to formulate an understanding of the role of the church in the world. A primary emphasis was placed on the missionary nature of the church, with this missionary nature being the basis of God sending the church into the world to participate in God's mission.

During the 1960s, some mission scholars were writing about the missionary nature of the church on the Protestant side,[64] but the focus tended to remain more on the discussion of the church's mission in the world[65] rather than engaging in a fuller reconceptualization of ecclesiology. In contrast, the Roman Catholic Church at Vatican II developed a more substantive understanding of ecclesiology in light of the missionary nature of the church.[66] But by the 1970s, the field of missiology was dominated by a conversation about the *missio Dei* and the kingdom of God. What is intriguing is the remarkable level of convergence that emerged by the 1980s around these concepts among ecumenical, evangelical, and Roman Catholic missiologists.[67]

Now after fifty years of wrestling with these issues, their fuller implications for our understanding of the church have begun to come into play. The substantive contributions of trinitarian studies in regard to mission are now being directed to the field of ecclesiology, i.e., an understanding of the church. There are two streams within trinitarian studies that inform this conversation.

The Western emphasis on God's one nature. One stream is represented by the theological tradition usually associated with the Augustinian tradition in the Western church. This stream tended to emphasize the one substance of the Godhead and focused more on God as absolute subject than as being relational. An example of this can be found in the work of Lesslie Newbigin.[68] The focus is on the sending work of God—God sending the Son into the world to accomplish redemption, and the Father and the Son sending the Spirit into the world to create the church and to lead it into participation in God's mission. This stream of trinitarian studies comes directly into the missional church conversation through the work of the Gospel and Our Culture Network,[69] especially, as noted earlier, in the widely read volume published in 1998, entitled *Missional Church: A Vision for the Sending of the Church in North America*.[70]

The Eastern emphasis on perichoresis. The Eastern church, especially the Cappadocian Fathers, placed an emphasis on the relationality within the Godhead—the interrelationships between the three persons of God. The social reality of the Godhead, in this approach, becomes the theological foundation for understanding the work of God in the world. Created humanity reflects this social reality of God through the *imago Dei*—humans being created in the image of God.[71] When this understanding is brought into conversation with the Western view of the Trinity, we begin to understand the church, through the redemptive work of Christ, as being created by the Spirit as a social community that is missionary by nature in being called and sent to participate in God's mission in the world. An earlier work that continues to be very influential in stressing this emphasis is by John Zizioulas, *Being as Communion: Studies in Personhood and the Church*.[72] A recent work that explores aspects of this Eastern view of a trinitarian approach is Miroslav Volf's *After Our Likeness: The Church as the Image of the Trinity*.[73]

These theological streams of trinitarian studies are contributing today to a renewed understanding of ecclesiology in relation to missiology. The fuller mission of God, understood as the *missio Dei*, is now being related to the redemptive work of God as best expressed in the kingdom of God. This relationship of God's continued work in all of creation being related to the redemptive work of God through Christ in relation to the kingdom provides the framework for understanding the nature, ministry, and organization of the missional church.[74] In developing a fuller perspective on the Spirit-led, missional church, it is helpful to explore the biblical framework regarding God's work in the world now in relation to both creation and redemption, even as the church awaits the eschatological future of the *not yet* of the kingdom of God.

A Biblical Framework for Understanding the Spirit-Led, Missional Church

The Old Testament story is about creation, fall, redemption, and the expectation of the day of the Lord. God's passion for the world is made clear throughout this story.[75] The whole world was created to be in relationship with God, but the fall devastated this design. After humanity's fall into sin, the story of redemption unfolds around God's continuing concern for the entire world. This is made clear through the various covenants that God initiated with the human community.

The Old Testament Covenants

There are a whole series of covenants in the Old Testament that provide us with perspective on God's mission in the world. These covenants start with Noah (the Noahic Covenant in Genesis 9) and extend through Abraham (the Abrahamic Covenant in Genesis 12, 15, 17), Moses (the Mosaic Covenant in Exodus 19), David (the Davidic Covenant in 2 Samuel 7), and the prophet Jeremiah (the New Covenant in Jeremiah 31). In each of these covenants God made it clear that the larger horizon of God's intention was always the world. It is especially important to understand that God lodged the particularity of redemption for the whole world in the selection and election of Israel.[76] However, Israel's election was never about privileged status, but rather about being selected for witness and service to the world. Israel was to be a "light to the nations" (Isa. 42:6; cf. 60:1–3) and a "city set on a hill" (Matt. 5:14; cf. Isa. 2:2–4). Their communal life was to bear witness continually to the redemptive purposes of God so that this redemption would be available to all. The whole world was always in view, that all the nations might come to know the living and true God.

God's covenants in the Old Testament are God's clear statement of intent that, in spite of the fall and our own sinfulness, God is not finished with the world. Redemption is not just about some special people being chosen as an end in itself. God's election of Israel as a particular people was for the purpose of bringing the good news about God to all the nations. Election in the Old Testament was for service, not privilege. Unfortunately, Israel often turned the focus of its election inward and built barriers to keep the nations out rather than constructing bridges to bring them in (Amos 9:7; Isa. 19:24).

The coming of Christ into the world is in direct continuity with God's intention in these Old Testament covenantal commitments. When Jesus announces at the Last Supper that the new covenant is coming into full reality through his death and resurrection, he proclaims that the forgiveness of sins is now available to all (Matt. 26:28). In Scripture, whenever the forgiveness of sins is announced, it always has the whole of the world in view. Being "in Christ" (2 Cor. 5:17) is never about privileged status but rather about being selected for witness and service to the world because "in Christ God was reconciling the world to himself . . . and entrusting the message of reconciliation to us" (v. 19).

Critical to understanding God's redemptive purposes is understanding that the universality of the Good News is always embedded in particularity. There is no abstract gospel. Gospel is always clothed in culture and comes to expression through particular people within particular contexts.

The implication that became clearer over time in Israel's history was that participation in God's redemption in the world, while anticipating the fully revealed kingdom of God, was more about suffering service than privileged status (see especially the role of the Suffering Servant in Isaiah 53–54). This is a lesson that comes clearly into focus when Jesus tried to help his followers understand that the role of the Suffering Servant of Isaiah 53 must precede the full revealing of the reigning King of Daniel 7. In Jesus's words, "The Son of Man came not to be served but to serve, and to give his life as a ransom for many" (Mark 10:45). This is the same lesson the *missional church* throughout the ages is called to indwell, a lesson which it has often struggled to embody. The gospel frees the church to live in a posture of vulnerability within the world such that this vulnerability often leads the church to the margins. All too frequently the church has sought to amass power at the center in order to build and to maintain domain, as seen in both the established and corporate forms of the church. This domain is often more about serving the interests of the church than being the church for the sake of the world.

The Kingdom of God in the Gospels

In the Gospels, one encounters the expectation that a movement is about to be born as a result of the announced presence of the kingdom of God in the person and work of Jesus Christ. As Jesus said, this kingdom is present in our midst: "The kingdom of God is among you" (Luke 17:21). It is to be received (Mark 10:15), persons are invited to seek it (Matt. 6:33) and to enter into it (Matt. 23:13), while also looking toward that day when they will inherit it (Matt. 25:34). The coming of the kingdom is about God's power confronting and defeating the power of the enemy, the evil one (Matt. 4:1–11).

Living into the presence of the kingdom, the redemptive reign of God in Christ, means that illnesses may be healed (Matt. 11:2–5; Mark 1:29–34), evil spirits may now be cast out (Mark 1:39), and natural circumstances may be changed (Mark 6:47–52), even as the poor hear the gospel of the kingdom as good news (Luke 4:18–19). In Scripture, Jesus used parables to explain the kingdom as a mystery that only some have ears to hear and eyes to see (Matt. 13:10–17). The Father gave the kingdom as a gift to the followers of Jesus, and accepting this gift radically changes the way one looks at material possessions (Luke 12:32–33). While the presence and influence of God's kingdom will grow dramatically in the world (Matt. 13:31–32), there are also many who think they are part of God's kingdom who will also miss it (Matt. 21:33–44).

Jesus announced that the time of the presence of the kingdom being made manifest in the world was now at hand, and that redemption would now be brought to bear on all of life and that it was his intent to invite everyone everywhere to repent and believe this good news (Mark 1:14–15). In order to spread this message, he gathered around himself followers who were to learn to "fish for people" (Mark 1:17). The expectation was that these followers would serve as the foundation of the church that Jesus would himself build: "I will build my church" (Matt. 16:18). Anticipating his death, Jesus prayed not only for his followers but also for all who would come to believe in him through their testimony (John 17:20).

Following his death and resurrection, as noted above, Jesus made it clear that his followers were to take the message of salvation, rooted in God's kingdom (the redemptive reign of God in Christ), to all people and to the ends of the earth and to bear witness to its truths in relation to all of life (Matt. 28:19–20; Luke 24:47). Jesus also conveyed to these followers that they would be led in this work and empowered to carry it out through the presence of the Spirit among them (Luke 24:49; John 14:25–26; 20:22). Jesus clearly anticipated that a movement (persons who later came to be known as "Christians"; Acts 11:26) and a new type of organization (what came to be called the church [the *ecclēsia* as a called-out community]) would grow out of the work of these followers as they were led and taught by the Spirit (Matt. 16:18; John 17:20).

In this regard, it is critical to understand the relationship of the biblical *imperatives* to the biblical *indicatives*. Matthew 28:19–20 is built around the key imperative "make disciples," but this imperative is premised on the fact that those receiving this expectation are already a changed community empowered by the Spirit. This is reflected in Matthew 5:13–14 where the believing followers are reminded that they are already the "salt" and "light" of the world. This is an indicative statement of fact. The same point is made in Acts 1:8, where the followers of Jesus are told that they "will be [Jesus's] witnesses." This is also an indicative statement of fact. To express it as a double negative: you cannot not be Christ's witness if, in fact, you are empowered, taught, and led by the Spirit.

The book of Acts becomes a demonstration of this new reality. It began at Pentecost as the intensive indwelling of the Spirit took place within the community of 120 believers gathered together in Jerusalem. And it quickly spread within a growing church that soon spilled over into the larger world. As developed in chapter 2, the ministry of the Spirit led this early church into the world to engage in both evangelizing and holistic mission (as will be developed in chapter 7). The church's responsibility to be involved in both aspects of ministry continues to this day. The missional church conversation is helping congregations recapture an understanding that the Spirit-led church is inherently missionary by its very nature.

Summary

In the biblical framework outlined above, the Spirit-led, missional church is identified as living between the times. It lives between the now and the not yet. The redemptive reign of God in Christ is already present, meaning that the power of God is fully manifest in the world through the gospel under the leading of the Spirit. But the redemptive reign of God is not yet fully complete as the church looks toward the final consummation when God will remove the presence of sin and create the new heavens and a new earth.

The kingdom of God, the redemptive reign of God in Christ, gives birth to the missional church through the work of the Spirit. Its nature, ministry, and organization are formed by the reality, power, and intent of the kingdom of God. Understanding the redemptive purposes of God that are embedded within the kingdom of God provides an understanding of the church being missionary by nature. The church participates in God's mission in the world because it can do no other. It was created for this purpose. This purpose is encoded within the very makeup of the nature of the church.

In this approach, ecclesiology, our understanding of and participation in the church, comes to expression and identity in relationship to God's mission in the world. The genetic code of the missional church means it is missionary in its very nature or essence. This means that congregations exist in the world as being missionary by nature. The self-understanding of such congregations is not first of all being established (that they represent the primary location of God's activity in the world) or being corporate (that they do something on behalf of God in the world), but rather their self-understanding is missional (they are a created social community of the Spirit that participates through the Spirit's leading in what God is doing in the world).

Congregations are created by the Spirit, and their existence is for the purpose of engaging the world in bringing God's redemptive work in Christ to bear on every dimension of life. In being true to their missional identity they can never function primarily as an end within themselves—the tendency of the self-understanding of the established church. In being true to their missional identity, missional congregations can never be satisfied with maintaining primarily a functional relationship to their contexts and communities—the tendency of the self-understanding of the corporate church. The missional church has a different genetic code.

CHAPTER 5

Spirit-Led Discernment and Decision Making

It had been several months since the council meeting at Faith Community when the issue of how to address the space needs had become so intense. Following that meeting, Pastor Ron introduced the council members to some resources to assist them in using a process for mutual discernment and decision making. At this month's meeting, the members of the council are now engaging the same space problem, but with a very different approach.

Evelyn opened the meeting with an extended devotional Bible study on Romans 12 and invited the council members to reflect together on how this passage might inform their decision-making process. After some reflective conversation, they came to a mutual understanding of the necessity of their becoming a corporate living sacrifice, of dying to their individual agendas, in order to be able to better discern the will of God for their congregation. A time in conversational prayer followed this discussion, during which everyone invited the Spirit to help them become such a living sacrifice.

John and Bill gave a report on the assignment they had been given, which was to do a SWOT (strengths, weaknesses, opportunities, and threats) analysis on the congregation and its ministry to its community. They presented a summary of information on both congregational membership patterns and demographic trends and then offered a summary SWOT of this data. Following this presentation, they invited their fellow council members to engage in a theological reading of this information in seeking to answer the following two questions: What is God doing? and What does God want to do?

During this discussion it became clear to the council that God was, in fact, at work in their context. Many persons were indicating a responsiveness to the gospel, and there were many of these that Faith Community was well situated to reach. In addition, there were several advocacy issues the congregation was involved in that appeared to be making a difference in the lives of many community residents. In order to better participate in what they understood God to be doing, they needed to be responsible, as one member put it, "to remove the barriers" in addressing their space problems.

As the implications of this insight began to come into focus, Harold observed that it would be important to bring the congregation into this conversation with the council. Evelyn, with a background in organizational development, offered some useful ideas for designing a process to help the congregation engage in its own discernment process of responding to the council's leadership. This process also addressed how to work through the changes that would be required by the vision that was beginning to come into focus for this congregation.

The evening's meeting closed with Pastor Ron leading a reflective devotional from Luke 14:25–33 on the cost of discipleship, followed by another session of conversational prayer.

In the midst of this complex world of diverse perspectives and competing worldviews, Christian leaders are called to lead.[1] The opening example of the Faith Community council illustrates that leading can be a challenging task. The diversity we now often encounter represents, to a large extent, the effects of the significant changes that have taken place over the past hundred years in how we understand and interpret what we know, which is usually referred to as our *hermeneutics*. The question now before the leaders of congregations is, In seeking to be Spirit-led, how can we provide leadership of Christian communities in helping them address critical issues? This chapter addresses this question, first, by introducing a general framework for understanding how Christian communities might engage in Spirit-led discernment and decision making, and second, by outlining a process for this engagement.

Engaging in ministry as a Spirit-led, missional church requires the leaders of congregations to engage in discernment and decision making. This presents a great challenge today in the midst of the complex world in which we now live. The changing pattern of immigration in recent decades has introduced the reality of diverse cultural communities into the midst of once familiar and usually somewhat homogeneous neighborhoods. The emerging postmodern condition continues to cultivate an environment where value choices and moral decisions, once taken to be black-and-white, are now seen as relative. The effects of radicalized modernity and the continuous technological changes that shape and reshape our shared lives—which therefore diversify any shared understandings—are now self-evident.

The Challenge of Leading in Mission in the Aftermath of the Hermeneutical Turn

Clearly, the council of Faith Community was seeking to employ a distinctively Christian framework to support the process they were using for their discernment and decision making in regard to how to address their space needs. However, before examining this framework and process in detail, it will be helpful to explore a bit further some of the complexities that Christian leaders face in seeking to lead Christian communities in mission.

From Method to Methods

In light of the hermeneutical turn that has developed over the past century,[2] there is no going back to a world that can be framed in seemingly black-and-white categories. The diversity of interpretations of reality, which are manifest both in the multiperspectival character of biblical studies and the different methods used by the social sciences, makes this impossible. This means that part of the challenge facing Christian leaders today is learning to engage diverse perceptions of reality by drawing on a variety of methods that can inform the discernment and decision-making process. Relying primarily on one method, whether it is in relation to biblical teaching or scientific explanation, is no longer viable, if it ever was. Diverse perspectives, rooted in different methods and the particulars of social location, bring a multiperspectival dynamic into any discussion. Rather than playing out these differences around power dynamics related to personalities, roles, or the vote of the majority, which is so often the case in congregations, a more redemptive approach is to engage such differences through a process of mutual discernment. This requires leadership. This requires time. This requires a mutual commitment among those who are around the table. And this requires being Spirit-led. Reflected in this approach is the important theoretical insight that we need to develop a practice of "communicative reason" within diverse communities in order to come to shared conclusions.[3]

The utilization of a diverse number of methods for discernment and decision making can be seen in the example of the Faith Community council. The council engaged in actively inviting the Spirit of God into their midst to guide their conversation. They incorporated data from the congregation and context to better inform their decision making. They drew deeply from biblical and theological foundations to frame their interpretation of their situation, and to come to an understanding of how to strategically participate in God's mission within their context. And they drew on theoretical insights from the social sciences to plan a process for engaging the congregation and implementing a change process.

These various sources of information—context, congregation, Scripture, theology, and social science theory, which are all made available through different methods—all contributed to a Spirit-led discernment and decision process. They illustrate how a variety of methods can help inform Christian leaders who are trying to make decisions. The process used to interact with and to utilize such diverse sources of information is also multifaceted. There are multiple ways to engage in discernment and decision making. One could start with information from any particular source and then interact in a variety of ways with other sources. The approach proposed in this chapter argues for Scripture to be used in an authoritative way. But when it is used and how it is incorporated into the discernment and decision-making process is as diverse as the sources of information available from the variety of methods that are used.

Keeping God in the Conversation

An essential dimension that Christian leaders must attend to in the midst of a discernment and decision-making process is how to keep God in the conversation.[4] It is this dimension that makes Christian discernment and decision making unique. This is especially true when this dimension seeks to incorporate God's perspective into the discussion. This is done both through accessing the teaching of Scripture and theologically reflecting on it as well as in allowing God to function as an acting subject through the presence of the Spirit of God working in the midst of the community.

Interestingly, a number of literatures have emerged over the past several decades that are related to this challenge of trying to keep God in the conversation. All of them reflect the hermeneutical turn in interpretation, and each offers insights into a Spirit-led discernment and decision-making process. But their approaches range across a wide spectrum, from seeing God as being directly involved as an acting subject to incorporating God indirectly by referencing a Christian perspective within the process. These various literatures are worth reviewing, in general terms, as an introduction to the approach that is proposed later in this chapter.

Rethinking theological education. Beginning in the early 1980s, a vibrant conversation surfaced among theological educators about the very nature of what constitutes *theological education*. This discussion was launched by Edward Farley in 1983 with his book *Theologia: The Fragmentation and Unity of Theological Education*.[5] He deeply critiqued the classic four-fold division of contemporary theological education (Bible, church history, systematics, and practical theology), noting its inadequacy to address the substance of theology. He also challenged its tendency to support the clergy paradigm of ministry with its focus on instrumental skills. This had earlier been most clearly conceptualized by H. Richard Niebuhr as the professional "pastoral director."[6] Farley's work gave birth to a lively debate, one which was quickly engaged by numerous authors. A helpful summary of this discussion is provided by Robert Banks in *Reenvisioning Theological Education*.[7]

While the details of this discussion are too extensive to include in this brief summary, it is worth noting some of the key authors and their contributions. These persons include Charles M. Wood, who emphasized theology as a process of critical inquiry;[8] Joseph C. Hough Jr. and John B. Cobb Jr., who tried to give more content to Farley's proposal by focusing on Christian identity;[9] the Mud Flower Collective, who brought a feminist critique to the conversation with an emphasis on story and the voice of the marginalized;[10] Joseph C. Hough Jr. and Barbara G. Wheeler, who placed the conversation into the context of the congregation in order to break free from the clerical paradigm;[11] Rebecca S. Chopp, who constructed an approach to theological education around feminist practices;[12] Max L. Stackhouse, who brought theological education into conversation with globalization, contextualization, and mission;[13] and David H. Kelsey, who reframed the "Christian thing" in theological education as an effort to understand God truly.[14] All of these authors were trying to frame an approach for keeping God, whether directly or indirectly, in the conversation about theological education. To do this, there was general agreement regarding the importance of collapsing the Enlightenment divide between theory and practice and with it the unnecessary and unfortunate marginalization of practical theology. The proposed reconstruction was toward finding some way to reintegrate theological knowledge (*theoria*) with practical wisdom (*phronesis*), and for these to be shaped by personal and communal formation (*habitus*).

Engaging in theological reflection. Another literature that has recently emerged that attempts to keep God in the conversation is that which emphasizes the importance of theological reflection. This stream also reflects the hermeneutical shift in thinking about God and Scripture. The general approach of these efforts to develop a method for theological reflection is to develop insight, perspective, and an understanding of what God is doing in relation to the concrete issues of life. The emphasis is on drawing on a number of sources to engage this process, which usually includes some combination of Scripture, tradition, experience, and reason.

One of the earliest books in this field was by James D. Whitehead and Evelyn Eaton Whitehead in 1980.[15] It brought the resources of Scripture, tradition, and experience into conversation with context and the concrete practices of ministry in a process of deep reflection. The effort was toward developing a theological imagination within a

Christian community for discerning the presence and work of God in its midst.

Others have contributed to this genre, such as Howard W. Stone and James O. Duke, who stress the importance of bringing the human and divine perspectives into creative conversation through a process of theological reflection.[16] They point out that reflecting on the concrete issues of life facing the church is usually the best way to begin such reflection. Another contribution along these lines comes from Patricia O'Connell Killen and John de Beer, who start from a more explicit anthropological perspective.[17] Theological reflection for them is more the result of insights into life which come from human reflection on life's experiences.

Doing theology in context. Another important stream of literature from the past several decades dealing with keeping God in the conversation comes from the field of missiology. There are several strains within this stream. One comes from Roman Catholic missiologists. In 1985 Robert J. Schreiter published what has become a seminal piece on this subject entitled *Constructing Local Theologies.*[18] Drawing deeply from key figures who contributed to the hermeneutical shift in the past century, especially the work of anthropologists, Schreiter develops a working model for how Christian communities in particular contexts construct a local theology. In essence, his model is an adaptation of the correlation approach (which had been introduced by Paul Tillich) of bringing the church tradition into dynamic conversation with culture, especially the local culture. Schreiter notes a variety of sources within his model that can serve as a starting point for the process.[19]

Stephen B. Bevans is another Catholic missiologist working in this area of doing theology in context. His primary contribution to the conversation was in noting the variety of models that are used in constructing local theologies. His key work, *Models of Contextual Theology*, first published in 1992 and updated and revised in 2002, offers the reader an overview of six different models.[20] These diverse approaches clearly reflect the transition to approaching human knowing from a hermeneutical perspective. All of them seek to find a way to keep God in the conversation, whether directly or indirectly, but they work from substantially different frameworks of understanding.

Parallel to the work by Catholic missiologists, there have also been contributions from Protestant missiologists in the area of doing theology in context. One of the more influential is Lamin Sanneh, who published a key volume in 1989 entitled *Translating the Message: The Missionary Impact on Culture*.[21] As noted in chapter 3, Sanneh keeps God in the conversation by working from the premise of the inherent translatability of the gospel, that the Scriptures can be translated into any and every cultural context. Using Christianity in Africa as his primary case study, he notes how the dynamic truths of Scripture are often set loose in new ways of understanding through the language, thought forms, and worldview of the recipient culture. And in turn, there is often a reciprocity to the process as these new insights loop back to reshape Christianity within the original sending culture.

Similar to Sanneh, British missiologist Lesslie Newbigin works with the dynamics of how Scripture and culture interact. Taking the incarnation as the key biblical referent for understanding how the gospel can become particular while conveying universal truths, Newbigin argues that the gospel always comes to us as a "scandal of particularity."[22] In this scandal, the particularities of local culture do not cancel out biblical truths, but, in fact, properly understood, make them more accessible to our finite understanding.

Focusing on Christian practices. Recently, another literature for keeping God in the conversation has begun to emerge around Christian practices. This literature explores the importance of Christian communities engaging in shared practices. A volume entitled *Practicing Our Faith*, edited by Dorothy C. Bass in 1997, stresses that these practices need to be rooted in the Christian tradition and that Christian communities cultivate an active awareness of the presence of God by practicing their faith within these shared practices.[23] Some twelve different practices are discussed by the various contributors, all of which stress the challenge of trying to understand the presence of God in the midst of the mundaneness and messiness of everyday life.

A more substantive treatment of this approach appeared in an edited volume by Miroslav Volf and Dorothy C. Bass in 2002. Here the various contributors offer a fuller framework for understanding the importance of Christian practices, which they define as "things Christian people do together over time to address fundamental human needs in response to and in the light of God's active presence for the life of the world."[24] The general direction of this pursuit is shared in common by the contributors. But the multiperspectival character of trying to interpret God's active presence is clearly evident in the diverse views offered for bringing theological understanding to the various Christian practices that are discussed.

Reimagining practical theology. During the past several decades, the hermeneutical turn has also impacted what is known as the discipline of practical theology. Practical theology has a long tradition in the church, with deep roots historically in the Roman Catholic Church where it became known as pastoral theology.[25] At that time, a curriculum was developed that dealt primarily with moral theology, ethics, spiritual formation, and confession.[26] Protestants, with their emphasis on Scripture, turned pastoral theology into a curriculum that included preaching, liturgy, pastoral care, catechesis, and diaconal service.[27]

An important shift took place through the work of Friedrich Schleiermacher in the early nineteenth century with his *Brief Outline on the Study of Theology*, when he set up theological education within the newly formed University of Berlin.[28] What had been pastoral theology now became the division of practical theology. This *other* division of the curriculum became responsible to apply the truths gained from the disciplines of exegetical, historical, and philosophical theology.[29] This Enlightenment divide between theory and practice has plagued practical theology ever since.

A more focused conversation about reframing practical theology within theological education also took place during the 1980s and 1990s. Two important contributors to this discussion are Don S. Browning and Gerben Heitink. Browning's key work, *A Fundamental Practical Theology*, attempts a reconstruction of practical theology through employing a revised critical correlation approach. In this approach, he argues for the use of practice-theory-practice in order to bring text and context into conversation with descriptive, historical, systematic, and strategic lenses.[30] His work clearly reflects the hermeneutical turn in that he proposes the use of multiple interpretive lenses in trying to understand the life and ministry of Christian congregations.

While his work is helpful in framing the multiperspectival character of engaging the task, his use of biblical and theological texts tends to be underdeveloped in shaping an understanding of a congregation's life and ministry. The limits of Browning's model and his hermeneutical framework become most evident when he engages his third case, the apostolic church of God. He affirms that a "vigorous hermeneutical conversation is present in that church" and notes that "the authoritative voice of the Scriptures is at the heart of this conversation."[31] However, it is clear that the way this congregation keeps God directly in the conversation is both beyond Browning's own comfort zone and outside of his preferred hermeneutical approach. At the heart of his hesitancy, there appears to lie the question of divine agency, the extent to which one can truly know God as an acting subject.

Another important reconceptualization of practical theology is available in Gerben Heitink's *Practical Theology*. He takes his starting point for this reconception in the development during the 1960s and 1970s of a theory of action, which recognizes the embeddedness of theory within all human action.[32] Drawing on this foundational insight and adding to it a theological understanding led him to propose thinking of practical theology as a *theological theory of action*. Such a theory of action has three domains: (1) an interpretive domain that addresses a hermeneutical understanding of texts, (2) an interpretive domain that seeks an empirical explanation of context, and (3) an interpretive domain which seeks to identify and implement strategic action.[33] He draws on the communicative action theory of Jürgen Habermas and the hermeneutical treatment of text and context by Paul Ricoeur to flesh out the fuller dynamics of his proposed theological theory of action.[34] This chapter draws substantively from this work but adds to it a more focused content regarding a hermeneutically framed, theological theory of action.

Spirit-Led Leading in Mission in Congregations in Light of the Hermeneutical Turn

The point being made above in relation to the various literatures that were reviewed is that understanding Christian leadership in congregations today requires an approach that works from the perspective of the hermeneutical turn. Such an approach to leadership involves at least four interpretive dimensions that need to be integrated into a common framework. These dimensions are the following:

- **Texts.** In seeking to lead in mission, Christian leaders accept the biblical record as authoritative. They also accept various documents resulting from the interpretation of that record (theology and confessions) in the history of the church as being authoritative in some way. This fruitful prejudice[35] means that Scripture is accepted in some way as having a normative role in shaping the life, choices, and practices of a congregation. This use of Scripture and the church's historical theological reflections on the faith provide a *biblical and theological framing* of the issues within the process of discernment and decision making.[36]

- **Context.** In seeking to lead in mission, Christian leaders take into consideration the influence of the social location of a congregation in relationship to its larger cultural context, often drawing on social science research to clarify and focus this influence for constructive purposes. The use of theoretical perspectives from the social sciences as well as insights from common wisdom provide for a *theoretically informed* understanding of the issues within the discernment and decision-making process.

- **Community.** In seeking to lead in mission, Christian leaders understand that a congregation as a community created by the Spirit has members who are in relation with one another. Such a community engages in multiple shared practices that reflect its Christian understanding and commitments.[37] As a Christian community they need to utilize a discernment and decision process to corporately confess the Christian faith and plan for the ministry of the congregation. Reliance on the Spirit's leading through a process of *communal discernment* maintains God's presence in the process as an acting subject.

- **Strategy/Action.** In seeking to lead in mission, Christian leaders make decisions to take strategic action in further shaping the shared life of the congregation. Such action would reflect the normative understanding of the texts, the insights acquired from research within the context, and the wisdom from shared practices within the congregation. Decisions that lead to choices means that the community of faith will engage in *strategic action* that is communally discerned, biblically and theologically framed, and theoretically informed.

The argument presented here is that Christian leaders can most effectively lead in mission in Christian congregations by integrating these four dimensions into a shared process and by understanding the hermeneutical nature of this process. Such an approach to Spirit-led leading in mission in Christian congregations brings these dimensions into conversation and integration in the form of communally discerned, biblically and theologically framed, and theoretically informed strategic action. While developed here as distinct dimensions, it is recognized that all of them weave in and out of one another. Also, while being presented here in a sequential fashion for the purposes of presentation, it is recognized that these dimensions are, in reality, highly interactive such that the process can find its starting point within any of these dimensions. The following alternatives illustrate this, where any of these six sequences can serve as a viable pattern for engaging in discernment and decision making.

Theology—Theory—Action	Theology—Action—Theory
Theory—Theology—Action	Theory—Action—Theology
Action—Theology—Theory	Action—Theory—Theology

The following figure identifies the interrelationship of these four dimensions. These dimensions need to be understood as being dynamic and interactive. One can start anywhere in the process and then involve the other aspects for discernment and decision making. There is, however, a telos intended, as illustrated in the direction of the arrows, which is to move toward strategic action.

Communally discerned. Leading in mission from a hermeneutical perspective involves a gathered Christian community, with the congregation being the most common public and organized expression of such.[38] This is where the disciplines of ecclesiology and missiology come together within an understanding of the missionary nature of the church, or what today is being referred to as a "missional church."[39] As noted earlier, an understanding of the missionary nature of the church received formative development in the 1960s among Roman Catholics, especially at Vatican II,[40] but was also developed by a number of Protestant theologians within the ecumenical movement.[41] Although displaced for several decades because of a focus on radicalized secularism, this conversation has resurfaced in the past

Fig. 1. A Theological Theory of Action

two decades in the work of Lesslie Newbigin and David Bosch, along with the Gospel and Our Culture Network in the U.S.[42]

A missional ecclesiology stands at the core of leading in mission in relation to a hermeneutical perspective. A missional ecclesiology understands congregations as being the creation of the Spirit.[43] As communities are created by the Spirit, so also congregations seek to be led by the Spirit. They do this by engaging in some form of a discernment process in order to understand their purpose (mission), and how they are being called through this purpose to participate in God's mission in the world (*missio Dei*). They explore and examine the texts of Scripture and their respective confessional traditions to determine how they believe God is leading them and what they believe God is requiring of them. They also explore their own identity as a Christian congregation to discern how God has been at work in their midst in the past in leading them into mission and ministry. This involves carefully examining the shared practices in which they engage as well as the shared history that they have experienced. The field of congregational studies has been particularly helpful in contributing approaches to this part of the discernment process.[44]

Congregations also engage in some form of decision process for making choices about what they will do to live out the commitments required by their purpose. In doing so, they often engage in research on their ministry location, as also represented by the field of congregational studies, to find ways of translating their understanding of the Christian faith in relevant ways for engagement within this context.[45] While this corporate process of discernment and decision making is common to Christian communities, it is by no means standard in terms of approach. Clearly, different denominational traditions approach this in diverse ways, as is formalized in their polities but also often reflected in their ethnic traditions.[46] Exploring such differences and their results would be an interesting subject to pursue, but goes beyond the scope of this present chapter.

All Christian congregations are situated in a perspectively interpreted world and as such need to be aware of the limits of how they make truth claims. There are two dimensions of Christian existence, however, which are available to inform and guide the process of discernment and decision making.

First, as noted above, the Spirit of God is present in the midst of the congregation. According to Scripture, it is the work of the Spirit to lead and to guide a congregation into understanding God's intent revealed in Scripture and to apply this to its local context.[47] This requires some form of communal activity, according to 1 Corinthians 12 and Romans 12. It is the Spirit who gives diverse gifts to individual members of a congregation, and through this diversity these members are responsible to come to a synergistic collaboration and shared understanding.

Second, it is the character of communal activity that, while being led by the Spirit, such activity also involves the complexities of different values, biases, interpretations, and power dynamics between members or groups within a congregation. How can congregations come to a common mind in the midst of such complexities, complexities that often involve conflict? Rather than engaging in strategies of win-lose, it is important that congregations learn the practice of communal discernment.[48] While there is a spiritual dimension to this, as noted above, there is also a cultural-historical dimension, one which is best approached from a hermeneutical perspective. Different interpretations of reality are embedded in the complexities of differences among members of a congregation. While not being naïve about human sinfulness and the power dynamics of persons seeking to control or subvert a decision process, there are ways to engage the discernment process both constructively and redemptively.[49] This is where critical theory contributes to the process with its ability to unmask hidden agendas and disproportionate power dynamics.[50]

Open, fair, engaging, and deliberative discourse is essential for such a process to become operative. Here, it is helpful to draw on the influential contribution of the theory of communicative reason.[51] In the face of our differentiated perspectives, being committed to engaging in deliberative discourse is essential for coming to a shared understanding. This concept from Jürgen Habermas is also found in the work of both Hans-Georg Gadamer and Paul Ricoeur and their emphasis on using dialogue to come to shared interpretive perspectives.[52] All of these theorists recognize the essential social reality of the interpretive process. When coupled with a Christian understanding of the Spirit-led nature of the discernment and decision process, Christian congregations are in a unique position to come to negotiated interpretations of reality and shared commitments in relation to the authoritative texts and their social context. But to do so, they must be willing to sustain a committed engagement of deliberative discourse—*communally discerned*.

Biblically and theologically framed. Leading in mission from a hermeneutical perspective in Christian congregations relies on understanding the texts of Scripture and their interpretation over time. It involves both historical studies of the texts as well as the development of particular confessional traditions within the historic Christian faith. The understanding of the texts, through the well-established interpretation of them by Christians over the past two thousand years, starts with the preunderstanding that these texts are authoritative and normative—the hermeneutical circle. This is an acceptable preunderstanding for those who are Christian, and the interpretive process can usually begin at this juncture, although the specific content drawn from the authoritative and normative nature of these texts is open for continuous deliberation. For those who are not Christian, this preunderstanding represents a difference of interpretation. Engaging this discussion is essential to consider, but goes beyond the scope of what this present chapter is proposing.[53] The focus here is on leading in mission from a hermeneutical perspective for leaders of Christian congregations.

As noted above, the specific content related to the authoritative and normative nature of the texts of Scripture and historical confessions is open for continuous deliberation. However, there are certain interpretive frameworks, which have been communally discerned by the church throughout the centuries, that function as a guide for Christian congregations as they seek to understand God's mission and their participation in it. The following six assertions are offered as a summary of the larger framework of God's story as represented within an understanding of the *missio Dei* in relation to the kingdom of God as discussed earlier in chapters 2 and 4. The premise is that God's story has profound implications for Christian leaders as they seek to relate the purposes of God in the world as revealed in and through Scripture to their particular congregations and contexts.

1. God is a Triune God—Father, Son, and Spirit, and these persons of the Godhead are in a perichoretic relation (the in-relation character of the three persons), representing a social reality within the Godhead.
2. God is a creating God who has a passion for all the world to be in right relationship with him in light of creation design. This is rooted in the perichoretic nature of God (the in-relation character of the three persons). God seeks to be in relational community with all people in his creation, and this intent of his is often referred to as the *missio Dei*—the mission of God in the world.
3. In the midst of sin that corrupted the world, God is a sending God who seeks to redeem, and who sent his Son, Jesus Christ, into the world to defeat the power of sin and bring about the possibility of reconciliation of all persons and the redemption of every dimension of life within creation. The church is to participate in this redemptive work of God by unmasking the powers that have already been defeated. But it is to do so through a ministry of suffering service and cruciform discipleship, a discipleship that is based on taking up one's cross and dying to self while living in the power of the resurrection.

110

4. This reconciling and redemptive work of God was announced by Jesus Christ as being present in the kingdom of God, which, as the redemptive reign of God in Christ, places a high Christology at the center of the *missio Dei*. This means that God is seeking to bring back to right relationship all that was lost in the fall, such that redemption extends to every dimension of human life and every aspect of created existence.

5. God is working out the *now* of this redemptive reign in the world through the work of the Spirit in relationship to a gathered community, the church. This church is called into reconciled relationship with the Triune God and with one another and is sent into the world to participate fully in God's mission. The church is therefore a *sign* to the world that the *now* is already present, a *foretaste* for the world of the eschatological future that has already begun and an *instrument* to share this good news with everyone everywhere.

6. The *not yet* of this redemptive reign will one day come to consummation in God's time, resulting in removal of the presence of sin within the world and the creation of a new heaven and a new earth.

These truth claims are framed from a missiological perspective. They understand God as being a missionary God who is passionate about the world in seeking to reconcile all things within creation so that all of life can flourish. A missiological perspective provides a helpful framework for Christian congregations to utilize as they seek to participate in God's mission in the world. The value of having such a framework can be seen by going back to the opening example of the council meeting of Faith Community. If they had reframed their question about solving their space problems within such a framework from the start, they would have been better able to engage in a discernment process to address their question several months earlier than they eventually did. In doing so, it would be imperative that they rely on the active leading of the Spirit in guiding them into a decision, a decision that needs to flow out of and be responsive to this larger framework of the purposes of God in the world.

These core truth claims within the historic Christian faith provide a basic framework that Christian congregations can use to understand their purpose in relation to God's mission in the world. While some Christian traditions may offer additional, or even some different truth claims, it should be noted there has been an amazing convergence around these core concepts across numerous Christian faith traditions in missiology circles in the past few decades.[54] In addition, while there are numerous details required to fully operationalize these truth claims within a congregation's discernment and decision-making process, it is critical that a congregation utilize such a larger framework as a foundation for framing an understanding of its purpose—*biblically and theologically framed*.

Theoretically informed. Leading in mission from a hermeneutical perspective within a particular context cannot be adequately addressed without giving attention to the insights and contributions from the social sciences. Ricoeur is especially helpful here in providing an understanding of the relationship between the interpretation of texts and the interpretation of a context as a text.[55] While scriptural and confessional texts provide helpful insights into understanding the context in which a congregation is located, these texts are not adequate to provide sufficient information about that context for making and implementing strategic decisions.

Insights and understanding gained from the social sciences provide such information. In this way, the communally discerned, biblically and theologically framed interpretation of a congregation's purpose needs to be theoretically informed by the perspectives available from the social sciences. But it is critical to note that information from the social sciences is not value neutral, since it also is always hermeneutically interpreted. What is important is to bring these theoretically informed perspectives that are hermeneutically shaped into conversation with the hermeneutically shaped, biblical-theological understanding of the purpose of the congregation.

There is much debate in the social sciences regarding how one is to understand the insights generated through social science research. The complexity of this is evident in the various quantitative and qualitative research approaches that are being used today.[56] Here is a place, however, where the biblical-theological framework provides some perspective on how to approach the insights learned from the social sciences. Christians understand the world as having been created by God, where God is desirous to bring this world into a reconciled relationship with himself. God takes the world seriously. Christians, therefore, actively engage the world through Christian ministry, and though they interpret it through a hermeneutical lens, they believe that this world can be truly known, though always perspectivally. This makes information available from the social sciences useful and contributive.

An example of this is the use of organizational theory to understand the dynamics of congregational life. A theory of preference for many today is an open systems perspective, an approach which studies the relationship between an organization and its environment. Within this framework, resource dependency theory is helpful to congregations for understanding their relationship to their context, where a congregation has to secure sufficient resources from its environment in order to maintain viability.[57] Relating this process to change theory is also helpful for congregations in learning how to respond to or adapt to changes that are taking place in the environment.[58] Each of these theoretical perspectives needs to be critiqued for its usefulness in light of the biblical-theological framework, but it is clear that such theories from the social sciences can be helpful to leaders for leading in mission in Christian congregations.

What is important for understanding leadership from a Christian perspective is to critique these contributions within a biblical-theological framework. God's mission in the world is not just one more option to consider in making choices about life. God's mission frames the reality of how Christian communities are to live out their lives. Understanding leadership requires careful attention to the empirical explanations provided by the social sciences—*theoretically informed*.

Strategic action. In the final analysis, action is required to implement decisions. Leaders must lead Christian communities to engage in some type of strategic action. Such action, however, must be understood as more than just method, technique, or application. Action represents the strategic choice of an intentional community that is trying to shape and give meaning to its collective life. This is where a theological theory of action comes into play.[59] All action has theory embedded within it. For Christian congregations, it is important to determine communally discerned strategic action that is both biblically and theologically framed as well as theoretically informed.

The proposal being made on this point is informed by the recently developed focus on Christian practices, which were discussed earlier.[60] Christian practices that express some aspect of the communal life of a congregation have embedded within them substantive theological commitments. These practices utilize symbolic representation as a key way for conveying these commitments both to participating members and to those in the surrounding context. For example, when a congregation engages in the practice of hospitality in relation to its various activities and events, where it openly and genuinely welcomes the *other*, it is conveying something of its understanding of God as a God of hospitality. It is also conveying its commitment to accept difference and to be open to learning from the *other*.

Often, for Christian communities, the discernment and decision-making process begins with some action or praxis that requires assessment, which in turn leads to deeper theological reflection and reshaped action. Action is not neutral. Action is not optional. Action is not just about applying some truth. For Christian communities, action carries within it deeply embedded commitments to theological perspectives that are wisely informed by theoretical insights—*strategic action*.

Further Defining the Discernment and Decision-Making Process

The previous section provides a framework for better understanding the dynamics of discernment and decision making. In this section, a more detailed process is presented that can be used by congregations for engaging in communal discernment and decision making to address particular issues. The key question is, How can Spirit-led congregations come to shared understandings and agreements on strategic action to address specific issues, action that is shaped by biblical-theological frameworks and informed by theoretical insights from the social sciences? In answering this question, it is helpful to refer to a key passage of Scripture that lays out Paul's understanding of how congregations are to engage in communal discernment for making decisions.

Developing a Biblical Framework

Romans 12 follows Paul's lengthy explanation of his understanding of the Christian gospel (chapters 1–8), and his interpretation

114

that this has always been God's message of good news because the true children of Abraham are children by faith (chapters 9–11). In chapter 12, Paul addresses the Roman congregation in terms of how they should now live in light of these mercies of God that have been given. The grammatical structure of this chapter is important to note. In verses 1–2, Paul uses a series of plural nouns and pronouns in relation to a variety of singular objects. Their corporate life is to come to expression as singular outcomes.

Plural Subjects	Singular Objects
your bodies	living sacrifice
your	spiritual worship/service
your	mind
you	will of God

latreia—worship/service (Old Testament referent)

dokimazō—discern, discover, debate, decide

Paul is inviting the Roman congregation to understand its unity in the midst of its diversity. By becoming a communal living sacrifice—a singular object, they corporately express true spiritual worship or service (*latreia*). The referent point for this Greek word *latreia*, is the Deuteronomic sacrificial system given to Israel by God through Moses. In the New Testament, living in reconciled relationship as a Christian community is the equivalent of all the elaborate procedures for service that were required of Israel. Paul is asserting that this relationally reconciled community should be able to come to a common mind in discerning the will of God. Such a process is suggested by the word *dokimazō*, translated as "discern," which often involves various dimensions of communication such as intentional debate, dialogue, and discovery in order to get to shared decision. This discerning process is to be an active engagement where the participants struggle through their differences to come to a common agreement.[61] In this way, they are better able to come to an understanding of the will of God, both that which is revealed generally in Scripture and that which is communally discerned and agreed to by a congregation within a specific context.

Interestingly, Paul shifts the language in verses 3–8 to singular pronouns and nouns that have singular outcomes. Here the focus is on helping the members of the Roman congregation recognize and celebrate the diversity of spiritual gifts by which each person contributes to the whole. When each is making a contribution, then the reality of becoming "members one of another" comes to expression, and they realize and experience their inherent unity in the midst of their diversity (v. 5). This communal discernment of the will of God by a congregation requires dialogue among reconciled members who bring their own perspectival contribution to the process. The intended result is their effective ministry to one another (vv. 9–13) and their effective service and witness to a watching world (vv. 14–21).

As noted earlier, this process assumes the presence of the Spirit to lead and to guide a congregation, through its leaders, into discerning the will of God in relation to its particular context and into making strategic choices to implement this understanding. The Spirit's leading involves the giftedness of all God's people, and this diverse giftedness, with its inherent multiperspectival views, contributes to the communal character of discernment and decision making.

Framing a Process

The following process is suggested as a way to operationalize the discernment and decision making required of congregations for leading in mission.[62] These steps assume that there are specific issues that must be addressed or problems which must be resolved, things that are regularly before Christian congregations. While these steps are discussed here in a sequenced manner, they are, in fact, interactive in character (indicated in the figure by dotted lines) and often fold back into one another in the actual discernment and decision-making process.

Figure 2 offers perspective on how a five-fold process of communal discernment interacts with the previously developed aspects that inform decision making. The arrows provide clarity on how this process unfolds.

Attending. This phase of the process involves giving careful attention to the context, both the context of the congregation and that of the larger community within its cultural milieu. The key question is, In light of the issue to be addressed or the problem to be solved, what can be learned from giving careful attention to the situation

116

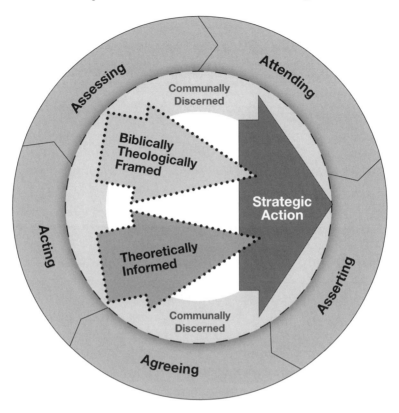

Fig. 2. The Five Phases of the Discernment Process

as it is presented? This is where the hermeneutical nature of human knowing comes into play. If communal discernment is utilized, there will usually be a variety of interpretive lenses used to try to understand what is going on. The goal is to achieve what Clifford Geertz describes as a thick description of reality.[63] Attending is the part of the process that includes both listening to the various perspectives, and also testing these against one another through using a type of triangulation process found in mixed-method research.[64]

It is important in this phase of the process to not prematurely engage in decision making regarding various interpretations. This can often be a difficult discipline to exercise in communal discernment within congregations since there often are persons who want to move quickly to take action because they believe the course of action is *obvious*. One other important dimension of the attending process in

Christian congregations is to read the interpretation of the situation from a theological perspective. In understanding God as an acting subject in the world, the following two questions, as introduced in chapter 3, are helpful in gaining a fuller perspective on God's presence and activity: What is God doing? (faith and discernment) and What does God want to do? (wisdom and planning).

Asserting. This phase of the process involves testing alterative strategic choices for action but doing so in relation to both biblical-theological frameworks and theoretical insights from the social sciences and common wisdom. It is critical to always assess potential action in terms of how it conforms to or might flow out of a biblical-theological understanding. This is where the texts function in an authoritative and normative way. It is also critical to bring theoretical information from the social sciences and common wisdom to bear on possible strategies. It is helpful to bring a variety of such perspectives into the discernment process so that the multiperspectival character of interpreting life and explaining a situation can be considered.

It is also helpful to consider a variety of strategic choices in the discernment process along with the possible implications of each choice. Sometimes the action of choice will be more tactical in nature and thereby have a shorter planning window for implementation. At other times the action of choice may be more systemic in nature, requiring a longer planning window.

Agreeing. This phase involves the process of coming to a communally discerned agreement on the strategic action of choice in light of biblical-theological foundations and theoretical insights. Foundational to this process for a Christian congregation is the role of prayer, which invites the active participation of the Spirit into the discernment and decision process. Attention should always be given to three things in coming to a communally discerned strategic action. First, the action should be intentionally founded in a biblical-theological framework so that in leading in mission there is a clear understanding available regarding how this action relates to or flows from God's mission and the congregation's participation in it. Second, the action of choice should be informed by the best available insights from the social sciences which bear on the strategic action that is being planned. And third, the implications involved in a strategic choice should be considered, relative to the amount of change required to implement it or the amount of disruption that it will most likely create within the congregation.

Acting. This phase of the process involves the implementation of the strategic choice that was communally discerned and agreed to. An implementation plan should have already been developed during the agreeing phase of the process and should include both action steps and a timetable. Usually, adjustments along the way in implementing a strategic action are necessary, which means that leading in mission requires constant attention for leaders of Christian congregations.

There are three dimensions that are important to the implementation process. These are (1) having a proactive communications strategy that keeps people regularly informed of what is happening, (2) providing active prayer that supports the action that is being implemented, and (3) engaging in regular feedback regarding progress being made, which allows for adjustments to the process when necessary.

Assessing. This phase of the process builds on the third dimension of acting that is listed above. It involves a thorough review of what took place in the implementation process of the strategic choice that was made. Efforts to learn from this process, both in terms of what worked and what didn't work, are important to consider. Depending on this assessment, a refocused strategic choice might be determined, which would take the congregation back through the process, starting with the attending phase. Or new realities that emerged in light of this previous strategic choice might need to be addressed through a process of communal discernment.

Summary

Developing a Spirit-led process for discernment and decision making and bringing this into the practices of leading in mission in a congregation are complex but essential tasks for Christian leaders. Doing so requires an awareness of the hermeneutical character of the interpretive process of determining choices for action and discerning what strategic action to take. It also requires a commitment to the communal nature of decision making within the interpretive process, one that is grounded in biblical-theological perspectives and that is informed by insights from the social sciences. Doing all of this requires an active dependence on the presence and leading of the Spirit. In the opening example of this chapter, the council of Faith Community utilized such a framework for addressing their space problem. In addition, they also utilized the initial steps in the discernment process, which were discussed above. Drawing on a framework such as this and developing a Spirit-led discernment and decision-making process in light of it, are foundational for Christian leaders who are seeking to lead Christian communities in mission. This is especially true for Christian leaders in the aftermath of the hermeneutical turn.

CHAPTER 6

Spirit-Led Leadership and Organization

It was the regular monthly meeting of the church session at Spirit of Life Presbyterian Church. All twelve elders were present, along with the two pastors. The major topic for the evening was the organization of the congregation, or more aptly put, its reorganization. Spirit of Life was ten years old and was continuing to show steady growth, with over 1,200 worshiping in its three services.

The organizational structure seemed to always be in flux. Following their Book of Order, the congregation had originally put into place a somewhat typical organizational structure, with the elders making up the session, plus a board of deacons and a series of six ministry committees. This model had proven to be cumbersome within a few years as rapid growth occurred. The session made some changes that are fairly typical today in fast-growing congregations, such as moving from committees to ministry teams and hiring staff to direct these teams.

The issue now before the session concerned how to balance a staff-led set of ministries with a session-led governance structure. Several elders were concerned that the staff appeared to have taken over decision making for the congregation. The two pastors were concerned that decisions be made in a timely manner on key issues and were finding the monthly session meetings to be inadequate for this purpose.

Finally, it was agreed that a task force should be formed with the mandate to study these issues and come up with recommendations.

They were asked to address the issues in light of Scripture, the Book of
Order, and the best thinking available from the social sciences.

The premise of this book is that the missional church is missionary
by nature—*the church is*. In living in the world, the missional church
engages in ministry that is consistent with its nature—*the church
does what it is*. Finally, the missional church seeks to bring order
and organization to these activities—*the church organizes what it
does*. It is the third aspect of the missional church that this chapter
seeks to address. What does Spirit-led leadership and organization
look like?

Spirit-Led Ministry Requires Leadership and Results in Organization

Chapter 2 illustrated the importance of biblically grounding our
conception of Spirit-led ministry. Chapter 3 explored the need to understand the contextual character of this ministry. This is especially
important, as discussed in chapter 4, given the development of the
denominational church over the past several centuries in the U.S.
A biblical understanding of Spirit-led ministry needs to be complemented with an understanding of Spirit-led discernment and decision
making as outlined in chapter 5. Together these foundations provide
the backdrop for beginning to explore the issues of leadership and
organization in the church.

As is too often the case, congregations, regional judicatories, and
denominations tend to start with restructuring the organization when
they seek to bring new vitality or renewal to the church. It is, however,
very difficult to renew a ministry from this starting point. Leadership
and organization in the church need to be understood as flowing out
of its nature, and, in turn, following from its ministry. This is where it
is important to keep in perspective that the church is always *forming*
and *reforming*. Leadership and organization need to be understood
as always being contextual and therefore always being provisional
in character. This means that leadership and organization will need
to change over time to respond to changing contexts. Unfortunately,
this has not been the case for many congregations and their denominations. The formal polities of churches that define leadership and

organization often end up hindering such development rather than helping to facilitate ongoing recontextualization.

The challenge of keeping leadership and organization supportive of ministry is present at all levels in the church. This needs to involve the interaction and integration of three sources of information as the church seeks to engage the dynamics of a changing context: (1) biblical materials, (2) historical polities, and (3) social science insights. Each source brings a significant contribution to the whole. None stand alone as being sufficient for understanding how leadership and organization should function within the church.

Biblical materials. The Bible provides a rich resource of information about leadership and organization. As the church in the New Testament spread into the world, it encountered a variety of different contexts and cultures. Quite naturally, the congregations that emerged in these contexts developed a variety of leadership and organizational approaches. The reality of this diversity is now evident in the different polities that make claims to alternative views regarding how the church is to be structured.[1] In the face of these competing claims about what the *right* form of church government is to be, it is evident that it is hard to argue successfully for a normative pattern for leadership and organization from the biblical materials. As an alternative to this, it is more helpful to recognize the variety of patterns and practices that emerged within the church during the first century. These need to be seen as being primarily contextual and provisional to those settings, although they certainly provide some perspective for the church through the ages to make its further decisions.

We find, for example, a number of ways that the church came to identify its official leaders. We find bishops, elders, and deacons in local congregations and apostles, prophets, evangelists, and pastor-teachers who ministered primarily at-large in relation to the leadership within congregations. Some of the mobile leadership roles that functioned more at-large continued into the second and third centuries, but by that time the focus had shifted to institutionalizing the church around bishops in relation to a variety of congregational offices such as pastors, elders, and deacons. Interestingly, few church polities that developed in light of the Protestant Reformation came back to recovering the mobility roles found in the early church. They opted instead to focus on a governance structure that provided for ordained offices in relation to a series of representative assemblies.

What is important to note about this variety of offices and roles is the necessity that there be formal leadership in the church. What needs to be seen as being contextual and provisional is the naming of particular offices, along with how they functioned. What is historically problematic in the life of the church is the way various streams of the church have settled on one interpretation of the pattern of leadership and organization as being normative throughout the ages for the church.[2] This introduces the important issue of historical polities in relation to leadership and organization.

Historical polities. Most seminary students learn before graduating the three basic forms of church polity that were developed over the centuries: Episcopal (governance through bishops), Representative (governance through representative assemblies), and Congregational (local congregational autonomy). These are usually taught from the perspective of the particular polity represented in the tradition of each seminary, where the merits of its polity are affirmed and the deficiencies of the others noted. The development of these polity traditions over the centuries makes it difficult to go back into the New Testament without bias. In light of being trained to think about polity through the lens of historical developments, it is hard to read the materials of the New Testament on their own terms and come to any clarity on how to proceed with matters of leadership practices and organizational structures. Power gets institutionalized within structure, and once structure is in place it is quite difficult to reform.

The church faces a challenging polarity. On the one hand, it needs to live out its inherent translatability into every context, and on the other hand it must avoid the pitfall of becoming overly contextualized (e.g., in Luther's day, the sale of indulgences represented a case of overcontextualization that he felt compelled to change; in our day, congregations face the challenge of not selling out to the values of consumerism even as they seek to demonstrate the relevance of the gospel to a new generation). Historical polities can helpfully inform this process. They provide clear examples of how the church's leadership and organization worked in other contexts. They provide an instructive understanding of various ways to read the biblical materials. And they provide helpful continuity with the past as the church tries to live into the future. The church does not start from scratch in any situation. It always brings with it an identity, ministry, and organization, which can helpfully inform both the *forming* and *reforming* of the church in new situations.

Social science insights. We have increasingly experienced, especially during the twentieth century, the influence of insights from the social sciences in understanding leadership and organization in the church. Pastors and church leaders often refer to the latest book that needs to be read for picking up on such-and-such an insight. Many of these are, indeed, quite helpful. But many times they are used without adequate consideration being given either to a biblical and theological critique or to how they interact with a historical polity and its practices.

Insights from the social sciences can be powerful. For example, the recently popular book from Jim Collins, *Good to Great*, has made the rounds of being read by many church leaders. His identification of what he calls "level 5" leaders is often noted as a key insight for application to church leadership and organization.[3] Unfortunately, one is not dealing with apples to apples when comparing level 5 leaders of great companies with effective pastors. In contrast to the CEOs of private, for-profit corporations, pastors must carry a week-to-week public role through their preaching where they represent God's presence and voice in the midst of God's people. The personality and skills that Collins notes regarding level 5 leaders may not correspond with all of those required of effective pastors.

An Overview of the Historical Development of Organizational Theory

The complexity of organizational expressions in the visible church, as noted in chapter 4, invites the necessity of developing some theoretical perspective. This is where the social science disciplines dealing with leadership and organizational studies can be helpful. They provide a variety of perspectives that can be used to study the church as a Spirit-led organization in relation to its context.

Some church leaders develop an explicit theory of leadership, but many do not. Instead, they function with some type of intuitive organizational theory or combination of theories for carrying out ministry. This usually reflects the combination of their previous work experiences, educational training, and personal reflection. But the congruence of such intuitive theories with the actual needs of a congregation is often inadequate for addressing the complexities of the congregation or the changing context that it faces. It is important for Spirit-led church leaders to develop a self-conscious organizational theory that reflects both the reality of the congregation's life as well as the complexities of the challenges before it.

Organizational theory, like many of the other social sciences, began to develop as a formal discipline in the early part of the twentieth century. The early theories, up until the late 1960s, are often labeled as being "closed system" theories. The reason for this is not that they were actually closed to their context or environment but rather that these theories did not take the context or environment into sufficient account in formulating their theoretical perspectives. It was usually assumed that an organization's functioning was largely self-contained within its internal life.

The implications of such closed system thinking for congregational life are readily evident among congregations facing rapid change today in their context, such as transition in the population makeup from ethnic immigrants. The seeming natural fit that a congregation once had with its local community is dramatically redefined as many members relocate to outlying suburbs and often transfer to other congregations. Church leaders in such a situation, coming at this issue from a closed system approach, usually attempt to address the problem with solutions that prove to be inadequate. These include such things as (a) searching for a pastor who can bring back the days of glory and success, (b) implementing internal ministries such as small groups and prayer strategies to strengthen member commitment, (c) developing ministries of service to the changed community but with no intent of enfolding any participants in the life and membership of the congregation, or (d) trying to develop a regional ministry profile that will attract persons to drive some distance to their location.

Such efforts may have some impact on strengthening member commitment along with attendance and participation for a time. But none of them, individually or collectively, are sufficient to address the more systemic issues facing the congregation. Such a discontinuous

126

change[4] in the composition of the community's population requires a more dramatic approach. Such a congregation must recognize that it cannot close itself off from its context and changing community if it hopes not only to survive but to also develop meaningful ministry. A Spirit-led congregation will learn to adapt and recontextualize its ministry to address the challenges and opportunities that it faces with such changes—always *forming* and *reforming*.

This understanding introduces the key insight related to an open systems approach in thinking about organizations. In approaching congregations from an open systems perspective, it is recognized that there is a dynamic relationship between a congregation and its local context. The more changes that occur in the context, the more adaptive a Spirit-led congregation needs to be to stay in *fit* with its community. What were once fairly stable neighborhoods in many communities are now dynamic locations of regular change. Responding to such dynamic change in a Spirit-led way requires a theoretical perspective that is able to incorporate such change within its understanding. An open systems perspective is helpful for providing this perspective.

Before developing in detail an open systems perspective, it is helpful to note some of the closed system theories that preceded it, all of which still offer some helpful insights. But it should be observed that all these theories pay inadequate attention to the influence of the context and also suffer from giving attention to a unit of analysis within an organization that is too limited in scope. The table below provides a summary of the key theoretical perspectives that can be labeled as being closed system in approach, along with the primary contribution of each approach.

Closed System Theories Early to Mid-Twentieth Century

Theoretical Perspective	Primary Contribution
Bureaucracy (early 1900s & 1950s)	Organizational structure
Scientific Management (1910s)	Supervision and efficiency
Administration Management (1920s–1930s)	Administrative process
Human Relations I (1930s–1940s)	Informal organization
Chester Barnard (1930s–1940s)	Organizations as inherently cooperative
Neo-Weberian (1940s–1950s)	Limits of rationality in adaptive bureaucracy

Theoretical Perspective	Primary Contribution
Human Relations II (1950s–1960s)	Changing people to improve organizations
Institutional School and Systems Theory (1950s–1960s)	Organizations as systems

Closed System Theories

Bureaucracy. Although he did not become influential in the U.S. until his work was translated into English after World War II, a turn-of-the-century German sociologist named Max Weber made some of the earliest contributions to formal organizational theory.[5] His primary contribution dealt with conceiving of *organizational structure.* He developed the concept of the bureaucratic structure as being an *ideal type.* This did not mean it was perfect but rather that it served as a conceptual construct for thinking about organizations. Drawing from his research on the Catholic Church and the new nation-state of Prussia, Weber's concern was to help organizations in the *modern* world shift away from arbitrary structures and discretionary decision making in their use of power and authority.

The key concepts associated with bureaucracy reflect the growing emphasis on *rationality* in light of the influence of the Enlightenment. Weber proposed that organizations develop the following:

1. Clearly defined division of labor with formalized positions.
2. Vertical authority centered at the top which could be formally delegated down into the system.
3. Defined rules and procedures that are adopted as policies in order to standardize decision making about rights and grievances.
4. Selection, promotion, and remuneration of employees based upon merit, technical competence, and job performance measured against clear criteria.
5. Formal channels of communication for the regular flow of information and decision making.

This theoretical approach to conceiving of organizations represented a significant improvement over many of the idiosyncratic organizations of Weber's day. Many of Weber's insights about structure are still quite helpful to note. The downside of focusing primarily on structure and formal authority, however, is that any organization is more than its organizational chart and policy handbook. The metaphor of "red tape" has also become descriptive of the problems often associated with bureaucracies in their standardized procedures. But this basic approach to thinking about congregations still holds much influence. Developing structure, defining procedure, and exercising authority are inherent to any organization. What is needed is to appreciate Weber's insightful contributions, while also incorporating these within a larger theoretical framework.

Scientific management. An early theory about organizations in the U.S. was introduced by Frederick Taylor in the early 1900s. Working as a consultant in steel mills, he used a scientific approach for conducting detailed time and motion studies to improve first line *supervision* in order to develop *efficiency* and to increase productivity. In 1911 he published his studies in *The Principles of Scientific Management*, which proved to be quite influential among business owners who managed these labor-intensive industries.[6]

It is important to note that Taylor's studies took place at the time when most heavy industry manufactory processes were still very labor intensive and where massive numbers of new immigrants often filled low-skill jobs. This accentuated the importance of direct supervision on the part of first line managers. The basic contributions of Taylor's work were:

1. The value of deskilling tasks into discrete and simple activities that could be performed by interchangeable individuals without much training or experience.
2. The clustering of work by functions to achieve more efficiency in the manufacturing process.
3. The importance of achieving efficiency through minimizing the motions required on the part of the worker to complete a task.
4. The necessity of direct supervision to keep workers on task in being productive.
5. The perception that individuals were motivated primarily by monetary rewards and would therefore work as isolated individuals to increase their own pay.

Taylor's work has been extensively critiqued for its limited focus within the organization and its naïveté regarding what motivates persons to work. Many of Taylor's basic premises, however, are still evident in the marketplace today in industries that require larger numbers of low-skill employees (e.g., the fast food industry). But perhaps Taylor's larger legacy is the attention he brought to organizational studies by emphasizing scientific inquiry and the use of research methods to explore the actual dynamics of organizational life.

Administrative management. One of the more familiar of the early twentieth-century organizational theories is known as administrative management. It emerged in the 1920s and 1930s in the midst of the increasing organizational character of modern life. Attention shifted away from the unit of analysis being the worker's performance on the manufacturing line to the *administrative process* that the manager employed to get work done within the organization.

This approach eventually led to the identification of a standard process that was assumed could be utilized by any manager in any organization. Such a process was proposed by Luther Gulick and L. Urwick in 1937 under the acronym POSDCoRB. This stands for the following: P—Plan, O—Organize, S—Staff, D—Direct, Co—Coordinate, R—Review, B—Budget. It was taken for granted that this process, once learned, could be used by any manager in any organization.[7] Over time, as other *principles* of management were discovered, they were added to the *normative* management approach that could be used by anyone under the assumption that there was *one best way* to manage within an organization. This assumption collapsed during the 1960s in the face of the growing complexity of organizations and the increased levels of change in the context. However, the importance of attending to the skills of the administrative process of managing people, tasks, and time continue to be necessary for those who would provide leadership in congregations.

Human Relations I. Another movement emerged during the 1930s that took organizational theory in a different direction, one that involved the *informal organization*. This became known as the "human relations school" of management and had its roots in the emerging discipline of psychology. It was made famous by the "Hawthorne" studies conducted by Fritz Roethlisberger and William J. Dickson along with Elton Mayo at Hawthorne Plant of Western Electric Company in Cicero, Illinois, between 1927 and 1932.[8] Researchers there attempted to study human motivation and to focus on both the formal and informal relationships within work teams. Through manipulating the physical environment of the conditions of the room in which a team of persons worked (e.g., the lighting intensity) and through use of control groups, they discovered that productivity went up in those rooms where the physical environment was being manipulated.

What they discovered was the importance of the *teaming effect*. As changes took place in their physical environment, the work team bonded in their informal relationships. This, in turn, led in turn to increased productivity in their shared tasks (the "Hawthorne Effect"). The importance of attending to the informal organization includes the following insights:

1. Persons are motivated by more than just monetary rewards in doing their jobs.
2. Informal group life is an important dimension of any organization.
3. Productivity goes up when people work together in teams around shared tasks.
4. The workplace is a social system that must be considered when developing an organizational theory.

This approach was later critiqued for problems in both the method used and the interpretation given. But these insights continue to contribute to our understanding of how the informal organization functions within the formal one, something to which congregations must attend.

Chester Barnard—transition figure. By the end of the 1930s, organizational theory began to find its voice as a social science discipline. Chester Barnard emerged as a spokesperson who consolidated many of the insights contributed thus far, while also anticipating future directions for this discipline. Barnard had served as president of the New Jersey Bell Telephone Company during the 1930s. His book *The Functions of the Executive*[9] was one of the first efforts to develop a comprehensive theory. He started with the assumption that organizations are *inherently cooperative* in nature. This meant that a manager, especially the top-level manager, was responsible to lead in such a way so as to elicit cooperation. This placed importance on several functions of the executive, including the following:

1. The importance of developing an effective communications system.
2. The importance of managing the human resources of the organization.
3. The importance of motivating employees to do their best.

This latter point is related to his *acceptance theory of authority*, which noted that while authority flows from the top down, it must be accepted by those it affects. This placed great emphasis on the moral example of the manager in shaping confidence and trust within the organization. Barnard's work anticipated several schools of thought that were soon to emerge within the growing discipline of organizational theory—the Neo-Weberian, Human Relations II, and Institutional/Systems schools. Interestingly, his emphasis on the inherent cooperative nature of organizations and the value of moral example by leaders are still of great importance for the church to consider in regard to Christian leadership.

Neo-Weberian school. By the 1940s and 1950s, new developments were taking place in communications technology and the development of massive organizational systems. In studying their impact, James G. March and Herbert A. Simon developed what became known as the Neo-Weberian school within the discipline of organizational theory. This theory focused on the *limits of rationality* as earlier proposed by Weber. They accepted the basic logic of bureaucracy but within that framework explored what actually went on inside of organizations, such as how managers made decisions in relation to how much information they had. They published their work in 1958 as *Organizations*.[10] The key contributions of their approach include the following:

1. Rationality in any organization is bounded, which means that there are limits on trying to achieve a fully rational perspective.
2. Decisions, therefore, can never be maximized, but rather decision makers have to satisfice how much information was necessary at what point to make a decision.
3. Efforts should be directed toward trying to change the premises for decisions rather than trying to change people.

4. Organizations have competing groups within them, vying over competing goals, which requires negotiation and compromise—what they labeled as the "garbage can model" of decision making.
5. People need to be socialized into the organizational culture of any organization.
6. The style of management is tied to and contingent upon the technology used in the primary processes of the organization.

These insights continue to inform organizations today and raise for the church important questions: To what extent is the church inherently cooperative and to what extent does it represent a competitive context of competing coalitions?

Human Relations II. This school stands in contrast to the previous theoretical perspective. It emerged in the 1950s and 1960s as the influence of psychology increased and the field of organizational psychology began to develop. Representative of this school are persons such as Douglas McGregor with his contrasting "theory X and theory Y" approaches to management,[11] Rensis Likert with his proposal for participatory management,[12] and Chris Argyris with his focus on trying to mature managers as individuals.[13]

The focus of these representative theorists was on trying to improve the quality of organizational life by *changing people* to function within organizations in healthier ways. In the midst of the broader egalitarian influences of the 1960s, there was a concerted effort to try to humanize and to democratize organizations through employing the following:

1. Emphasis on the importance of cooperation as the basis of working together.
2. Emphasis on training people to improve their abilities to function in more effective ways in the organization.
3. Emphasis on participation as the key to securing ownership and support of ideas and the work of the organization.

These insights are still important to consider for those seeking to provide leadership in the church. The question to address is, As a body of diversely gifted people, to what extent should the church focus on developing and changing the behaviors of people as the basis of nurturing community and shaping ministry?

Institutional School and Systems Theory. Another important development took place in the 1960s, when systems thinking began to find its way into the discipline of organizational theory. Ludwig von Bertalanffy introduced this perspective into the social sciences in the late 1940s through his work in biology and ecosystems, where it soon became known as General Systems Theory (GST).[14] It now became important to consider the whole of the organization and to incorporate all of the separate units of analysis of previous organizational theories into a more comprehensive approach.

Influential in this work were two figures: Philip Selznick and Talcott Parsons. Selznick developed his theory from his study on the organizational system of the Tennessee Valley Authority.[15] Parsons was a sociologist whose theoretical work included organizational studies.[16] His major contribution was in conceptualizing the complex character of modern organizations from a systems perspective. In doing so, he developed the Structural/Functional school of sociological theory, one that has been critiqued as overly legitimizing the status quo as being functional. The key themes that emerged from the work of these early systems thinkers are the following:

1. Systems are always displaying adapting behaviors in an effort to achieve integration.
2. Social systems display levels of stratification in terms of differentiated roles.
3. Function is determinative of structure within a dynamic system.
4. All social systems seek to accomplish some goal(s).

It is commonplace today to think of organizations, including congregations, from a systems perspective. This perspective, however, has been further developed, as noted below.

Open Systems Perspective

A significant paradigm shift took place in the late 1960s within the discipline of organizational theory with the introduction of an open systems perspective. This perspective added the dimension of the interaction of the organization with its context or what is usually referred to as the "environment." The tumultuous changes taking place in the 1960s—a globalizing economy along with the civil rights movement, youth culture, Vietnam War and anti-war movement, feminist movement, and ecological movement, required this shift in thinking. A number of works conceptualizing an open systems perspective were published at this time, including James Thompson, *Organizations in Action*;[17] Paul R. Lawrence and Jay William Lorsch, *Organization and Environment*;[18] and Daniel Katz and Robert L. Kahn, *The Social Psychology of Organizations*.[19] The basic conceptualization of an organization as an open system was framed around the components of inputs, transformation, and outputs.

The conception of a congregation as being in an open system relationship with its community/environment is displayed in figure 3. What is important to note is the dynamic relationship between the congregation as an organization within its larger context.

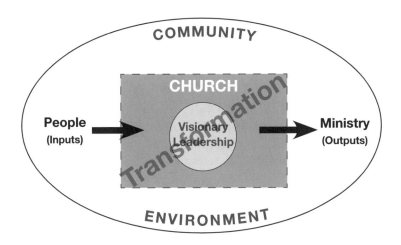

Fig. 3. An Open Systems Perspective

The premise of an open systems way of viewing things is that all organizations secure valuable and often scarce resources from their environment, which are then processed and transformed by the organization into some type of product or service and, in turn, are distributed back into the environment. Concepts like *fit* and *gap* became part of the language—to what extent is an organization in *fit* with its environment or, conversely, where are the *gaps* between what an organization seeks to do and its relationship to its environment? In addition, the notion of *organizational effectiveness* began to take its place alongside the former emphasis on *organizational efficiency*.

The open systems perspective has proven to be theoretically dynamic over the past thirty or so years. A whole series of theoretical movements within organizational studies have drawn on it to frame various emphases for the further development of organizations. Summarized in the table below are the more important developments.

Development of the Open Systems Perspective, 1970s to Date

Theoretical Perspective	Primary Contribution
Organizational Survival (late 1960s–1970s)	Gathering sufficient resources to survive
Goal Attainment (1970s–1980s)	Strategic planning
Reengineering and Continuous Improvement (1980s)	Total quality management
Transforming Organizational Culture (1980s–1990s)	Leaders developing vision
Learning Organization (1990s)	Systems and feedback loops
Postmodern (1990s–2000s)	Information technology, new science, and chaos theory

Organizational Survival. The initial emphasis of thinking about organizations as open systems interacting with their environments dealt with organizational survival. The key issue in question was, Can an organization secure sufficient resources to survive? It was assumed that if the answer was yes, then that organization was, at least to some extent, being effective. It soon became clear, however, that when survival becomes the primary goal of an organization, something has then been lost or diminished in terms of its rationale for existence.

We find many congregations today, when they face substantial changes in their contexts, that turn to survival as their reason for continuing to exist. They often employ desperate strategies of trying to secure sufficient people and financial resources to hang on. Included in this, for many such congregations, is a reliance on financial assistance from the regional judicatory or its national church body. This usually ends up being a stopgap measure that does not lead to long-term renewal. While it is essential that an organization survive in order to carry out its work, it has become clear to most organizational theorists that survival, in itself, is not a sufficient reason for existence.

Goal Attainment. The limitations of focusing on survival as being a sufficient goal led to an emphasis being placed on goal attainment. This was developed within an open systems perspective in the late 1970s as a process that became known as "strategic planning."[20] Strategic planning was used to help organizations clarify their purpose for existence and then to develop strategies for carrying this out. An organization would be considered effective if it could identify what needed to be accomplished and to make sufficient progress toward these goals.

Many congregations began to incorporate strategic planning into their organizational life by the 1980s. They found it helpful to clarify their purpose and then develop goals and strategies for carrying this out. The use of various forms of strategic planning continues to the present time, but its limits are increasingly coming to be recognized in the midst of the emerging postmodern condition. What is important is for the leadership of congregations to learn to think and act strategically, but to do so more in relation to taking a *journey* than trying to arrive at a particular *destination*. In this framework, goals are replaced by missional commitments that are implemented in flexible ways within a changing context.

Reengineering and Continuous Improvement. By the 1980s, another emphasis emerged in thinking about organizations as open systems. This is what became known in several ways, both as "reengineering"[21] and as "total quality management" (TQM).[22] The emphasis within this perspective was on utilizing a process of continuous improvement for redesigning the internal operations of the organization to insure higher levels of efficiency and productivity. Reengineering took the former silos that grew out of an emphasis on structural/functional differentiation and integrated them within horizontal processes. Total quality management was used to invite persons at every level of the organization, usually in teams, to find ways to improve on the work being done.

Many congregations have picked up on this emphasis around the theme of promoting *excellence* in their implementation of various ministries. There is a focus on searching for ways to continuously improve what they are doing. One drawback of this approach is that it can become overly concerned with internal operations and limit the attention given to the external environment. But putting in place processes for attending to continuous enhancement of ministry is an important issue that congregations need to consider, especially when they find themselves in dynamic and changing contexts.

Transforming Organizational Culture. This represents a fundamental shift from the primary role of a manager to the work of a leader. The hermeneutical turn discussed in chapter 5 began to have an influence on how organizations were viewed in the 1990s. Insights from social anthropology, in particular, were important for introducing a new understanding regarding how humans make meaning. The focus shifted to the *culture* of the organization as a whole,[23] and to a view of leadership as an activity of *sensemaking*.[24] This contributed substantially to the shift taking place in the 1990s from an emphasis on managing to a focus on leading.

The activity of leadership became increasingly viewed as an activity of sensemaking in shaping and reshaping the organizational culture through (a) identifying and promoting core values, (b) clarifying and focusing the mission/purpose, and (c) developing and casting a shared vision of the future. This emphasis on values, mission/purpose, and vision has proven to be a powerful tool for those seeking to lead congregations. It has become clear that in contexts where congregations are in need of being revitalized, leaders find it helpful to utilize this approach of identifying values, clarifying mission/purpose, and articulating vision. However, what needs to be added to this from a missional church perspective is an emphasis on understanding the nature of the church that the Spirit has created.

The Learning Organization. Focus on an organization as a learning system also entered the conversation about organizations as open systems in the early 1990s. This was popularized by Peter Senge in his book *The Fifth Discipline* in which the fifth discipline was the necessity of using a systems perspective in understanding the organization.[25] This required building in feedback mechanisms that allow for regular organizational learning. This was largely a nuanced understanding of a former insight regarding feedback loops within open systems. But with this insight, organizational thinking moved in a new direction, with organizations becoming proactive as learning systems in using information feedback loops for purposes beyond evaluation and assessment of results.

Some congregations have been able to adapt a learning systems perspective into their organizational life. They recognize the importance of being flexible and adaptive in being able to respond to change (e.g., many congregations have shifted away from formal committees to the use of more flexible task forces or ministry teams). However, many congregations are hampered in utilizing this approach by the inflexibility of the polity that is part of their denominational identity. Bringing historical polities into conversation with a learning systems perspective is an item that has still not reached the agenda for many denominations and their congregations.

Postmodern. This category involves a number of different influences that are continuing to reshape our understanding of organization and leadership, including such things as information technology, the new science, and chaos theory. While placing these various dimensions into one category is potentially problematic, they are all representative of another paradigm shift now taking place within the discipline of organizational studies. This is typically identified by the concept of the postmodern. The scope and pace of change being experienced today, enhanced by the rapid expansion of information technology, is requiring dramatic changes in how organizations are conceived and in how they function. New metaphors are being tested in efforts to bring comprehension to the character of organizations. Some are being drawn from the field of new science, especially chaos theory, as illustrated in Margaret Wheatley's book *Leadership and the New Science*.[26] A whole new literature regarding the impact of information technology on organizations has emerged, characterized, for example, by Bill Gates's book *Business @ the Speed of Thought*.[27] This has led to conceiving of organizations more as networks than as bounded entities.[28] Related to these influences is the growing awareness of the influence of the emerging postmodern condition on all of life in the U.S. As discussed in chapter 5, this means that there is now an awareness of the perspectival character of all human knowing.

In the midst of these developments, congregations are being challenged to find fresh ways to articulate and live out the gospel even as they seek to steward the historic Christian faith in dynamic and changing contexts. Attending to leadership practices and organizational structures in pursuing this task is of critical importance. So how should congregations proceed to think about leadership and organization today? With this question, we return to the issues presented at the beginning of this chapter: the interrelationship between biblical materials, historical church polities, and social science insights in relation to contextual realities.

Spirit-Led Congregations, Organizational Theory, and an Open Systems Perspective

Spirit-led congregations are organizations. However, as discussed in chapter 3, they have a duality to their nature in being both holy and human. This means that the study of congregations as organizations must bring together biblical and theological foundations in relation to social science insights. It is clear that significant developments continue to take place in the discipline of organizational theory. It is also clear that there are some frameworks and theoretical approaches that continue to be of help in thinking about organizations. One of these is the use of an open systems perspective. While the dynamics of the emerging postmodern condition along with the influence of chaos theory and informational technology need to be taken into consideration, their influences can largely be accounted for from within an open systems perspective.[29]

For these reasons, the approach presented in the remainder of this chapter considers a Spirit-led congregation in relation to an open systems perspective where biblical and theological foundations are utilized to reflect on the social science insights from organizational theory. Taking this approach, what might be called a "missional approach," allows for the following:

1. This approach allows for an examination of the congregation as a whole and provides a framework within which to consider every dimension of the congregation's life and ministry.
2. This approach provides a way to integrate biblical and theological perspectives with the dynamics of the organizational life of congregations.

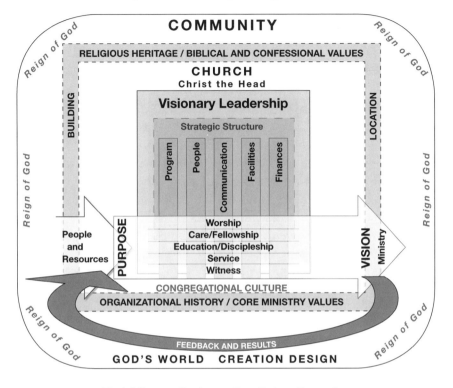

Fig. 4. A Congregation from an Open Systems Perspective

3. This approach provides helpful concepts and tools for describing the complexity of a congregation while seeking to understand the dynamics of life within this complexity.

4. This approach allows for taking seriously the world as God's creation and the purpose of the church in participating in God's mission in the world within the framework of understanding the relationship between an organization and its environment.

5. This approach allows for thinking about congregations as both always "forming and reforming" in relationship to a changing context while stewarding a congregation's identity within the historic Christian faith.

6. This approach allows for utilizing both core organizational metaphors and biblical metaphors for understanding the life and ministry of congregations.

141

The approach that follows takes major components of thinking about a congregation as an organization within an open system and integrates biblical and theological perspectives with each component. The method used introduces each component and then integrates it within a progressively built diagram that displays the interrelationship of all the components. *This framework is intended to be used as a diagnostic perspective for conceiving the complexity of congregational life and being able to plan and implement ministry in relation to this complexity.* The full diagram, except for the final dimension, is pictured in figure 4 on the previous page, and then this diagram is developed piecemeal fashion in what follows (i.e., figures 4.1–4.6 along with their corresponding sections).

Community/Environment. To understand Spirit-led congregations from an open systems perspective it is important to start with the context, which is the *community* or what is usually referred to as the *environment*. Biblically and theologically we see the world as

Fig. 4.1. Community/Environment

God's creation within which God is at work bringing redemption to bear on every dimension of life. This is where God's intent within creation intersects with the cross through our integrating the redemptive reign of God in Christ—the kingdom of God, with the *missio Dei*—the mission of God. The *reign of God* is operative everywhere within the context.

God's world as God's creation design is represented in every community/environment, and any changes taking place within this social and cultural context need to be a matter of interest to a congregation. Spirit-led congregations have a dynamic relationship with the communities they seek to serve. On the one hand, there are many forces within the community/environment that shape or influence a congregation. On the other hand, a congregation seeks to influence aspects of its community/environment. The primary way of theorizing this relationship is from the perspective of "resource dependence theory."[30] Congregations must be aware of the resources they need to draw from their environment in order to carry out their purpose and accomplish their vision. The primary way of theologizing this relationship is in terms of how a congregation is called, gathered, and sent to participate in God's mission in the world—for the sake of the world.

The types of information that a Spirit-led congregation should be interested in gathering about its community include such things as population trends, demographic profiles, transportation patterns, residential location of membership, organizations serving the community, business development and employment, and so on. It is important not just to gather such information but, as pointed out in chapter 2, to read this information from a theological perspective as congregations and their leadership ask the questions (a) What is God doing? (faith and discernment) and (b) What does God want to do? (wisdom and planning).

Congregation/Boundaries. The next component of thinking about a Spirit-led congregation from an open systems perspective is to examine the boundaries that give it an identity within its community. This concept of boundaries is important to understand, for in many ways congregational life is about managing the boundaries. First, it is important to realize that the boundaries are perforated (represented in the figure by dotted lines), which means that people as well as a congregation's influence can, and do, flow in and out through

Fig. 4.2. Congregation/Boundaries

its boundaries. The congregation is an open system interacting with its community/environment. Another key concept is that boundaries help to shape a congregation's identity. A congregation is more than a location and a building. It is a community of people who live under the lordship of *Christ* as the *head of the church*.

There are four types of boundaries, two that are physical and two that are social-cultural-historical. The two physical boundaries are the *location* of where the church gathers and the *building* or *facilities* that it utilizes. Typically, a congregation builds a facility to house its activities. The location as well as the architecture of this facility, or any facility which is used by a congregation, represent important boundaries. Both the visibility and accessibility regarding location are foundational. The principle regarding buildings is that once we shape our buildings, our buildings then shape us. This needs to be considered in the design and use of physical space. Congregations would be well served by conducting a focused analysis of the space utilization of their facilities to better enhance their ministry.

The other two boundaries are social-cultural-historical in character. The first is the *religious heritage* and the *biblical and confessional values* that are embedded within the congregation's existence. So many congregations that are part of historical traditions, in seek-

144

ing to become relevant, often downplay this part of their identity. They do so to their own loss. A congregation's identity is deeply tied to its story. Learning to tell this story in fresh ways is critical, but telling the story is essential. Related to this is the other boundary of *organizational history* and *core ministry values*. Every congregation develops its own organizational history, which often is greatly influenced by the various pastors who served the congregation. Learning to read this history like a book that is still being written, where the various chapters are identified in terms of themes and even titles, can be helpful. The key question to ask is, What is the chapter we are presently in or the next chapter the Spirit is leading us into? The ministry values embedded in the congregation's story are also helpful to clarify. It is important to ask, How congruent are our practices of ministry with the values we hold about ministry?

Taken together, these boundaries begin to shape a *congregational culture*. This represents the atmosphere of the congregation in terms of what people experience. It is helpful for a Spirit-led congregation to give attention to shaping the congregation's culture to represent more faithfully and fully the purposes of God in the world.

Feedback and Results. A Spirit-led congregation as an open system is always interacting with its community/environment. This means that there is always a flow of activity on both sides of the life of the congregation—*people and resources* are flowing in, and *ministry* is flowing out. It is essential for congregations to attend to the feedback loop of information regarding how these flows are functioning. The questions to consider are, What is happening at the front door? and How is the congregation impacting its community/environment?

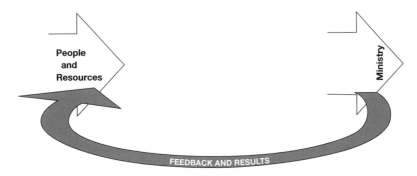

Fig. 4.3. Feedback and Results

Too often congregations rely on anecdotal or episodic information to assess what is happening.

To answer these questions in a constructive way, congregations find it helpful to set up feedback loops that are both systematic and systemic. Being systematic means that a congregation is seeking to develop feedback loops that can provide a more comprehensive picture of what is happening. To be systemic means that congregations are looking for the underlying issues that are shaping things the way they are. From an open systems perspective, an organization is always searching for information, both *feedback* on what is happening and the *results* or outcomes of what took place. From a theological perspective, it is important to learn to guide this process through being intentional about cultivating Spirit-led ministry.

Purpose (Mission), Core Missional Practices, and Vision. These three dimensions of a Spirit-led congregation are essential for understanding why it exists, what it is to do, and how the Spirit appears to be leading into the future. The first element, *purpose*, which is often referred to as *mission* in the literature, has to do with why a congregation exists. The key question to answer is, In light of the missionary nature of the church, why has God called this congregation into existence? The answer to this question comes from Scripture. Spirit-led congregations do not start from scratch in trying to figure out their purpose. God has already made clear what congregations are to be and to do. They are to be a community of God's people called, gathered, and sent to bear witness to the redemptive reign of God as they seek to participate in God's mission in the world.

Interestingly, many congregations define their purpose around the things they do such as worship or educating or witnessing, and thereby miss a deeper understanding regarding why God has called them into existence. A congregation's purpose has to find its expres-

Fig. 4.4. Purpose (Mission), Core Missional Practices, and Vision

sion in relation to what God has done and is doing. What is important is keeping the focus on the larger horizon of how the congregation understands its purpose and identity in relation to God and God's activity in the world through the ministry of the Spirit.

The second element involves the *core missional practices* of a congregation that represent the primary ways in which a Spirit-led congregation carries out its purpose. In the organizational literature, these are typically referred to as the "technologies" that an organization uses to accomplish its purpose.[31] From a theological perspective, these represent practices that Scripture indicates are normative for all congregations. They typically include (a) *worship* (which includes Word and sacrament ministry), (b) *education/discipleship*, (c) *care/fellowship*, (d) *service*, and (e) *witness*.

Each of these missional practices requires some type of organized activity in order to be implemented as a structured program. The style and manner of developing programs can vary greatly between congregations and will be influenced by both historical traditions and culture contexts. This is the place where much of the controversy within congregations takes place—over matters of style and preference. A Spirit-led congregation needs to inform this discussion with the understanding that the church is always both *forming* and *reforming*.

The third element to consider is *vision*. Vision has to do with how a congregation discerns the Spirit's leading into the future. Whereas Spirit-led congregations look to the *Bible* to define their *purpose*, they look to their *context* to discern their *vision*. Vision in a congregation is a Spirit-led discernment process of coming to a shared understanding of what God is doing and what God intends to do in its particular context. There is an eschatological dimension to vision. It is a reflection of a congregation living in both the *now* and the *not yet* of the kingdom of God. Vision has a shelf-life. As times change, it is used up. Both biblically and in the organizational literature, vision is a key element for effective leadership. Learning to cast vision is a skill set that leaders need to develop.

Leadership and Infrastructure. Intersecting with the core missional practices that carry out a congregation's purpose as it seeks to live into the vision God has given, are the exercise of *leadership* and the development of organizational *infrastructure*.

Fig. 4.5. Leadership and Infrastructure

At the heart of the life and ministry of a Spirit-led congregation stands the critical aspect called *visionary leadership*. Chapter 5 discusses the importance of this in regard to discernment and decision making. What is important to note here is the essential role that Spirit-led leadership plays in developing, forming, and guiding congregational life and ministry. The emphasis here is on *leadership* rather than *leader*. Visionary leadership involves a large number of persons in both formal and informal roles who help shape a congregation's ministry. But visionary leadership also comes to formal expression in and through a strategic structure.

Designing a *strategic structure* is the first aspect of developing an effective infrastructure. This dimension of the organization needs to give direction to and provides oversight for all the rest of the infrastructure. Some polities already define in fairly detailed ways what this structure is to look like, who can serve, how they are to be elected or selected, and what their responsibilities are. Unfortunately, many of these formal requirements originally dealt with a church that was reforming in the midst of the Protestant Reformation and reflect many of the biases of a territorial, state church that had domain. It is critical to bear in mind that structure is the framework for how power becomes institutionalized.

It is important for Spirit-led congregations in dynamic and changing contexts to balance the requirements of reforming with the realities of forming. For example, many congregations have found it helpful to downsize the number of leaders that serve as the primary decision-making body. They have also shifted many of the operational decisions for the implementation of ministry to others in the system, whether staff or volunteer roles. Other structural changes in congregations include changing committees to ministry directors or ministry teams, developing a role around volunteer coordination for the entire system, and writing job descriptions for every task in the church.

There are various aspects of infrastructure that congregations need to develop, all of which need to be integrated with the core missional practices under the oversight of the formal visionary leadership that make up the strategic structure. One important dimension of infrastructure is *program*. Program represents the organized ways in which the core missional practices are carried out in a congregation's ministry. Every congregation uses some type of program as a regular part of its life. What is crucial is for a Spirit-led congregation to design, develop, and implement programs that faithfully serve the purpose of the congregation in relation to its core missional practices. An interesting characteristic associated with program is the extent to which style, time, format, and location often become sacred to many people. While this is not unique to congregations as organizations, it is probably enhanced due to the association often made between a particular program and the biblical practice that it is designed to carry out. What needs to be seen as being biblical is the practice itself, but unfortunately, the program is often substituted for this horizon.

Another dimension of infrastructure is *people*. This refers to all the participants in the life of a congregation. Theologically, people represent the body of Christ and the priesthood of all believers in a local congregation. This gives meaning regarding how persons relate to one another and also gives direction as to how they find their place within the ministry of the congregation. Spirit-led congregations find it helpful to utilize some type of intentional welcoming and enfolding process that brings persons fully into the life and ethos of the congregation. They also find it helpful to have some type of intentional development and deployment process for utilizing people's gifts. It is important for such congregations to help all their members understand their vocation in the world as an integral part of their gift-based deployment for participating in God's mission in the world.

Another dimension of infrastructure is *communication*. It is crucial for Spirit-led congregations to develop capacity for sharing information, especially in a context where people's lives are divided up into so many different worlds of activity. Communication, properly utilized, can help to instill trust and to cultivate a healthy congregational culture. One of the symptoms of a sick system is when the rumor mill becomes a primary way in which people are receiving much of their information. This information is usually selective or distorted, or both. Congregations need to be proactive in building their communication systems, using a variety of mediums to convey information (e.g., text, visual, and audio) and a variety of formats (e.g., bulletins, print newsletters, email newsletters, message screens, and phone calling).

Another dimension of infrastructure is *facilities*. Facilities, as noted earlier, represent one of the key boundaries for a congregation. The design of church facilities has undergone substantial change in recent decades. How space is used today is different from the way that many buildings built prior to the 1970s were designed. Spirit-led congregations have discovered the importance of having a welcoming and gathering space that allows for people to congregate and interact. The importance of placing a spacious, pleasantly decorated, well-secured nursery close to the auditorium or sanctuary has also become a given for many congregations. And having readable and visible signage is essential, such that it allows anyone to navigate the facilities, from the parking lot to every internal activity.

A final dimension of infrastructure is *finances*. It takes monetary resources for congregations to function. Similar to facilities, there have also been significant shifts in how people give to congregations in recent decades. People are more inclined to give to *people* and specific *projects* than they are to a general *operational budget*. Many congregations have found it helpful to develop a program budget to replace the line-item approach, where the total costs associated with running each ministry area in the life of the congregation are listed. They have also found it important to provide members with regular feedback on what their monies are being used for. But the most important premise that Spirit-led congregations continue to discover about finances is that money follows vision. People more willingly support a plan that is presented to them in terms of what is believed to be God's future for the congregation.

Holy Spirit Guiding Transformation. The final dimension of thinking about Spirit-led congregations from an open systems perspective is a theological one. It is the recognition that it is the Spirit's ministry to bring about changed lives, transformed communities, and redemptive ministry in the world. This again reflects the duality of the church as an organization that is both holy and human. God desires congregations to live fully into the redemptive reign of God in Christ. This is the work of the Spirit in the midst of the congregation and through the congregation into the world. As noted in chapter 2, a congregation that is being led by the Spirit will sometimes experience as much change from interruption, disruption, and surprise as through planning and strategizing. This is important to remember when addressing the issue of transformation under the leading of the Spirit. While a Spirit-led congregation needs to work at identifying what it means to be effective in ministry so it can plan and strategize accordingly (wisdom and planning) it also needs to continue to maintain an openness to the work of the Spirit in its midst in unexpected ways (faith and discernment).

The full development of this perspective is displayed in the following figure. Here it is important to note that the transforming ministry

Fig. 4.6. Holy Spirit Guiding Transformation

151

of a congregation being led by the Spirit involves both its inner life and its participation in God's mission in the world.

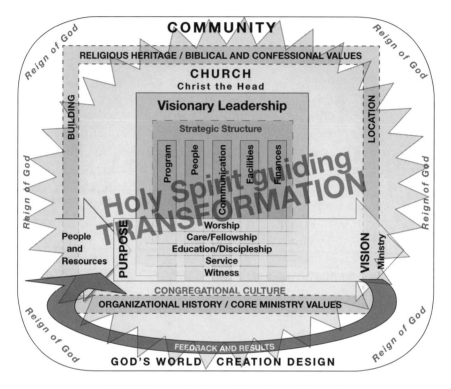

Fig. 5. A Congregation from an Open Systems Perspective with Transformation

Summary

The development of leadership and organization in the life of a congregation is a complex task and a dynamic process. It requires that careful attention be given to Scripture, a church's tradition and polity, and to insights from the social sciences. Engaging in development of leadership and organization will, of necessity, introduce change into the life of a congregation. Helping a congregation respond to change in redemptive ways and learning to guide the process of change are important leadership skills that need to be acquired. This introduces the focus of the next and final chapter.

CHAPTER 7

Spirit-Led Growth and Development

For several months, the council of First Church had been discussing how it might make the morning worship service more friendly and hospitable to visitors. After lengthy discussion, they finally voted to introduce an informal time of greeting prior to the official beginning of worship. This was announced the next Sunday and began the following week. People were asked to take opportunity to greet someone they didn't know or hadn't seen in some time and to have a few moments of conversation.

Two weeks into this new approach, the folks who came early and who normally sat in the back of the auditorium began to circulate a petition seeking to end this "disruption of the service," as they saw it. By the third week, representatives of this group visited the pastor at his home, presented the petition, and insisted that the council change the decision that had been made. Interestingly, this group had even gotten a visitor to sign their petition.

The council met in an emergency session later that week and decided to withdraw the decision they had made five weeks earlier. At their next monthly meeting, council members engaged in some reflection on this experience. Two insights emerged. First, someone noted that they appeared to have given away their power as a council in capitulating to a vocal minority in the congregation. Second, another person observed that they had likely also given away the issue of introducing any further changes in worship, and that it would be a long time before they would have the freedom to try to introduce any other innovations.

Introducing change can sometimes bring disruption. As illustrated in the example above, failing to adequately prepare the congregation for the change being introduced greatly compounded this sense of disruption, at least for some. Congregational leaders need to attend carefully to the *dynamics of process* when introducing change. Likewise, they need to help a congregation develop *capacity to respond* to changes taking place within its ministry and the community/environment it seeks to serve. This is where viewing a congregation from an open systems perspective, as presented in chapter 6, can be helpful. It provides a framework that can be utilized for addressing the dynamics of either guiding planned change, or responding to unanticipated change. But before proceeding with a discussion of these issues, it is important to gain some biblical perspective on change in relation to the growth and development of the church.

Biblical Perspectives on Change in Relation to Growth and Development

Chapter 2 introduced the ministry of the Spirit in relation to creation, re-creation, and the final consummation. Each of these aspects of God's working in the world introduces the importance of understanding change in relation to the ministry of the Spirit. In the garden, prior to their fall into sin, Adam and Eve were responsible to interact with the creation in furthering its development (subdue the earth and have dominion; Gen. 1:28). They were also responsible to bring into existence a growing human community through bearing children (be fruitful and multiply; Gen. 1:28). Both of these activities would inevitably introduce change into their lives. Living within a dynamic, changing world is part of God's design for human life.

This reality continues within re-creation, although here we encounter additional dimensions to human existence. Now the human community, made up of sinful persons, lives in the midst of a fallen world. But it still retains the responsibility to be stewards of all of creation through interacting with it and developing it. We also find that within this human community, those who believe in the living and true God have the presence of the Spirit to empower redemptive living and to cultivate transformed behavior. All of these dynamics are perhaps best summarized in the prayer that Jesus taught his disciples to pray: "Your kingdom come. Your will be done, on earth as it is in heaven" (Matt. 6:10). In praying this prayer, the believing community is, by implication, asking this question: Lord, how would you have us change in order to live more fully into the eschatological future that you desire to already make present in the world? A congregation in praying for God's kingdom to come has to recognize that in doing so, it is inviting itself into experiencing and participating in change.

We find, then, that encountering change is inherent in what it means to be human, and it is also inherent in what it means to be Christian. The church should expect to change as it interacts with its community/environment. The church should expect to change as growth and development take place through its ministry. And the church should expect to change as the Spirit works to bring about transformed lives living out of a new nature. It is interesting to see how these dynamics unfolded in the life of the early church as presented in the book of Acts.

Growth and Development in Acts—A Lens for Interpreting the Book

As introduced in chapter 2, the church regularly engaged in carrying out the Spirit-led ministries of evangelizing and mission. The author of Acts makes it clear that these ministries led to the growth of the church and its further development. In fact, the growth and development of the church in Acts appears to be a *lens* that the author is providing the reader for understanding the ministry of the Spirit in the life of the church. As the ministry of evangelizing everyone everywhere unfolded, we find the following references related to the *growth of the church*:

Acts 1:8 "You will be my witnesses."

Acts 2:41 "That day about three thousand persons were added."

Acts 2:47 "And day by day the Lord added to their number those who were being saved."

Acts 4:4 "But many of those who heard the word believed, and they numbered about five thousand."

Acts 5:14 "Yet more than ever believers were added to the Lord, great numbers of both men and women."

Acts 6:7 "The word of God continued to spread; the number of disciples increased greatly in Jerusalem."

Acts 9:31 "Meanwhile the church throughout Judea, Galilee and Samaria . . . was built up . . . [and] it increased in numbers."

Acts 11:21 "The hand of the Lord was with them, and a great number became believers."

Acts 12:24 "But the word of God continued to advance and gain adherents."

Acts 13:48–49 "As many as had been destined for eternal life became believers. Thus the word of the Lord spread throughout the region."

Acts 14:1 "A great number of both Jews and Greeks became believers."

Acts 14:21 "After they had proclaimed the good news to the city and had made many disciples . . ."

Acts 16:5 "So the churches were strengthened in the faith and increased in numbers daily."

Acts 17:12 "Many of them therefore believed, including not a few Greek women and men of high standing."

Acts 17:17, 34 "[Paul] argued . . . in the marketplace every day with those who happened to be there. . . . [S]ome of them joined him and became believers."

Acts 18:8 "Many of the Corinthians who heard Paul became believers and were baptized."

Acts 19:10 "This continued for two years, so that all the residents of Asia . . . heard the word of the Lord."

Acts 19:20 "So the word of the Lord grew mightily and prevailed."

Similarly, development also regularly occurred in and through the church in Acts. This took place as the church participated in God's larger mission in the world through the ministry of the Spirit. Consistent with the ministry of the Spirit, as presented in chapter 2, this resulted in God's redemption being brought to bear on all of life. It is interesting to note that many of these developments in the church grew out of the cross-cultural character of the ministry into which the church was led by the Spirit to engage. As discussed in chapter 3, it is often through contact with the *other* that new insights into how to participate in God's mission in the world come into focus. The following examples from Acts illustrate the *development* taking place in light of this larger mission of God to everything in the community/environment.

Acts 2   As the gospel was shared in households with slaves and masters their relationships to each other changed as both encountered Christ and then had to reencounter one another.

Acts 2, 4   Those with excess resources sold these things in order to share with those in need.

Acts 6   The leaders heard the communal complaint and addressed injustices in the distribution of food to the Gentile widows.

Acts 6   As Jewish priests became Christians, their whole life orientation in relation to Judaism was redefined.

Acts 9   As Samaritans became Christians, their social status was redefined in relation to Jewish Christians.

Acts 9   Becoming a Christian led Dorcas to do good deeds and acts of charity on behalf of those in need.

Acts 15   The race relations between Jewish Christians and Gentile Christians were redefined by the gospel.

Acts 16   Paul's relationship with Lydia helped to redefine the role of women in relation to church leadership in light of the gospel.

Acts 19   The church in Ephesus challenged the underlying religious, social, and economic structures through its alternative practices, resulting in significant cultural change.

The Church Encountering Change in Acts

This interpretive lens of the growth and development of the church in the book of Acts anticipated the expansion of the church that would continue to take place throughout the ages. In the midst of this growth and development of the church, there are indications that some intentional strategies were used. However, as noted earlier, the actual growth and development of the church under the leading of the Spirit was often introduced as a result of conflict, disruption, interruption, and surprise. We find examples of both planned and unplanned developments in the book of Acts, although the latter are more evident.

Growth and development from **conflict** *in Acts 6.* The Christian Hellenists complained because their widows were being neglected in the daily distribution of food. This complaint led to a decision to add additional leadership for managing the ministry of the church. This resulted in expanded ministry, which in turn facilitated even more growth taking place such that even many in the priesthood became Christians.

Growth and development from **adverse circumstances** *in Acts 8.* Jesus had made it clear that the apostles were to go from Jerusalem to the ends of the earth, but they kept staying in Jerusalem. Finally, a persecution scattered the disciples throughout Judea and Samaria, although interestingly, the apostles still remained in Jerusalem. The disruption caused by this persecution led, initially, to substantial growth from among persons whom Jewish Christians tended to look down on—the Samaritans (who were viewed as less than fully human by many of the Jews).

Growth and development from **ministry on the margins** *in Acts 11.* A further result of this persecution led some of the Gentile converts to Judaism, who had later become Christians, to return home to Antioch. There they started sharing the faith directly with other Gentiles without requiring them to adopt Judaism in order to become Christians. This ministry was a surprise to the church in Jerusalem. Following the Jerusalem Council, this understanding eventually became the foundation for the mission to the Gentiles and redefined both the gospel and the church in the New Testament period. What began on the margins came to the center.

Growth and development from **intentional strategy** *in Acts 13–19.* Being sent necessitates that strategic choices be made. After being sent out by the church at Antioch, Paul and those working with him made it a regular practice to win converts in the synagogues from among the Jews of the Diaspora as the foundation for planting reproducing churches in key commercial centers of the various provinces of the Roman Empire. As churches were planted, the missionary team would then move on to the next province, working their way westward.

*Growth and development from **divine intervention** in Acts 16.* In working their strategy of taking the gospel to the next province to the west, Paul and the mission team were blocked by the Spirit from entering both Asia and Bithynia. In the midst of this inability to continue to implement their planned strategy, God redirected the team through a vision Paul received to come over to Macedonia. This divine intervention, which required them to cross the Aegean Sea from the east to the west, shifted the location of the planned strategy for the planting of additional churches in other provinces.

*Growth and development from **new insights into gospel and culture** in Acts 10 and 15.* Peter's understanding of the gospel was dramatically reframed first by an encounter with God in a vision and then with Cornelius, the Roman centurion. While Peter wanted to claim that certain practices were theologically grounded, God made it clear that they were, in fact, culturally bound. What God called clean was to be understood as clean. Peter's strategy, in light of his understanding of a gospel that was clothed in the ceremonial practices of Judaism, would never have taken him to the Samaritans or to Cornelius. God intervened to disrupt and reframe Peter's understanding of both the gospel and culture, although Peter still continued to struggle for some time with fully accepting Gentiles as fellow believers in Christ.

In all but one of these examples, the church encountered significant change that was neither planned nor anticipated. In only one case was a strategy in place that directly led to the growth of the church. In the rest of these examples, the church was led by the Spirit in unanticipated ways to move in new directions. And each time, this resulted in growth and development taking place. Two patterns are evident. First, it is important to have a planned strategy that can lead to growth and development, as illustrated in the work of Paul's mission team. But second, there is also the Spirit's leading of the church through conflict, disruption, interruption, and surprise into new and unanticipated directions that result in growth and development. It is essential to have a strategy, but it is also essential to be alert to the disruptions and interruptions of the Spirit.

159

Accounting for Sin and Brokenness

Any assessment of the growth and development of congregations requires that one account for the reality of sin. As discussed in chapters 2 and 4, the missional church understands the world as fallen, as being disrupted by the presence of sin that is pervasive throughout all creation. This includes the presence of sin in the church, in general, and also within congregations as particular local expressions of the church. There are a number of ways in which an open systems perspective can be utilized in developing a biblical and theological understanding of how the presence of sin in congregations interacts with the ministry of the Spirit.

The presence of principalities and powers in the world—context. Congregations should expect to encounter the presence of evil in their context. This is evident in the brokenness encountered in people's lives as well as by the injustices and oppression in the social-cultural-institutional context in which they minister. Theologically, this is where ministering from the perspective of the cross, often from the location of suffering service, comes into play. Jesus made it clear that as his disciples we should expect no less. A Spirit-led congregation should expect to be misunderstood, and even mistreated, as it seeks to do good in the name of Jesus. Living into the redemptive reign of God in Christ within its context, a congregation will seek to announce the good news of the reconciling power of God to bring back into right relationship every dimension of life. While many will welcome and accept this as good news, others will resist and oppose it, since the gospel requires that persons change.

The presence of principalities and powers in the congregation. Just as evil is present in the world, so also evil is present in the church. It is important to remember that the church is both holy and human; in like manner people are both simultaneously saints and sinners. While redemption is possible in every area of life, sin is still present in the church in all of its terrible ugliness along with the brokenness that the effects of sin can cause. According to Galatians 5:22–23, a congregation is empowered to live out of a new nature by a new set of values—"love, joy, peace, patience, kindness, generosity, faithfulness, gentleness, and self-control." These are the corporate fruit of the Spirit. But people in a congregation are also capable of living by

160

the values of the old nature—"fornication, impurity, licentiousness, idolatry, sorcery, enmities, strife, jealousy, anger, quarrels, dissensions, factions, envy, drunkenness, carousing, and things like these" (Gal. 5:19–21). Anyone who has lived for any time within a congregation is all too aware of how many of these latter behaviors often manifest themselves in congregational life.

It is critical that those who provide leadership in a congregation not be naïve regarding this reality. Being able to discern and name the powers that disrupt the life of congregations is a critical skill to be developed by leadership in the missional church. Congregations should anticipate that they will experience internal disruption stemming from sin and brokenness. Knowing how to redemptively confront this is essential. But it is also important that persons providing leadership be able to identify and name their own shortcomings. This is where grace through forgiveness becomes the basis of effective leadership in the missional church.

Cooperative or competitive? One of the points noted in chapter 6 regarding the history of organization theory was the different perspectives regarding organizations. Are they to be understood as primarily *cooperative* in nature or fundamentally *competitive*? For the church and for congregations, the answer in many ways is *both/and*. The ministry of the Spirit is to bring about unity in the midst of diversity—a diversity which many times involves genuine differences of opinion. As discussed in chapter 5, coming to a decision in the midst of such diversity requires both patience and a willingness to negotiate and collaborate. There are times, however, when the competitive side of organization life gets embedded within the realities of the old nature. In this case, strife and conflict are not uncommon. While those providing leadership in congregations must be careful not to name differences of opinion too quickly as being a problem, they must also not be naïve about the reality of how sin can organize itself into unredemptive uses of power in the decision-making process.

Understanding resistance to change—homeostasis. A critical lens for understanding how congregations function from an open systems perspective is to note how they inherently tend to resist change. The behaviors of people, once they become what sociologists call the *norms* of an organization's life, tend to become institutionalized in terms of peoples' expectations.[1] Once a pattern or behavior has been established, an inherent resistance emerges that resists changing it to something else. Interestingly, this is even true about behaviors that are openly acknowledged as being dysfunctional or harmful to the life of the organization. Persons seeking to provide leadership in congregations need to realize that every change they seek to introduce will at some point be met by an equal level of resistance. Sometimes, the manifestation of this resistance is delayed. For example, it is not uncommon for a congregation that has adopted a plan for change, one that even enjoys wide support in the congregation, to be systematically dismantled over a period of several years as leaders rotate. It requires high levels of intentional commitment and investment of energy to both make and sustain planned change in congregations. The more complex and systemic the change, the higher the level of intentionality and energy that is required.

Addressing the question of transformation. There has been significant theological controversy over the centuries regarding the issue of spiritual transformation. Theological views range from total and unchangeable depravity to complete and sinless perfection in regard to the Christian life. The view offered here takes a position between these perspectives, and follows the understanding of all Christians being simultaneously saints and sinners. While redemptive change is possible and expected in terms of people's behaviors and practices, the full reality of sin is never diminished in terms of being present. The very process of grace and redemption that leads to transformed behavior is the same process that continues to make us aware of our own sinfulness and shortcomings. This is why humility is an essential Christian virtue.

Being Faithful and Effective in Relation to Spirit-Led Growth and Development in Congregations

One of the important concepts developed in relation to using an open systems perspective to understand organizations is *effectiveness*. As noted in chapter 6, many of the earlier organizational theories tended to emphasize efficiency. Understanding organizations from an open systems perspective placed a parallel emphasis on the importance of effectiveness. In simple terms, an organization was considered to be effective when it accomplished certain things consistent with its purpose.

In dealing with congregations, this is an important issue. But we need to add to this discussion the importance of congregations also being *faithful*—being faithful to bear witness to the kingdom of God and to participate in God's mission in their context. It is important to think about congregational faithfulness, effectiveness, and efficiency from a biblical and theological perspective as well as from an organizational perspective.

Clarifying purpose and renegotiating a congregation's vision. As mentioned in chapter 6, all congregations as organizations seek to accomplish something. These goals, whether formal or informal, reflect a congregation's explicit or inherent understanding of its purpose. This is why it is so important that the purpose (mission) of a congregation be grounded in what God has revealed in the Bible. God has already made it clear what the purpose of a congregation is to be. What is important for those seeking to provide leadership of congregations is to reflect continually on God's purpose for congregations and to bring this understanding fully into the life and ministry of the congregation in developing a Spirit-led vision for the future. This is often a process that unfolds over time. While God's purpose for congregations does not change, a congregation's comprehension of that purpose will go through growth and development over time. Congregational faithfulness, effectiveness, and efficiency, then, involves a congregation defining God's purpose and discerning God's vision for the future in its life and ministry.

Restructuring a decision-making coalition. In organizational theory, the concept of a decision-making coalition is usually referred to as the "dominant coalition."[2] Because of the connotations associated with the word "dominant" for a congregation, the language of "decision-making coalition" is being used here. Such a coalition represents the confluence of both formal and informal decision makers in shaping the outcome of shared decisions in the life of a congregation. Those seeking to provide leadership in congregations need to be alert to both of these—the formal leaders as well as the informal, for both are involved in affecting the outcome of decision making. As a congregation comes to increased clarity regarding its purpose and its vision of how to participate in God's mission in its context, it is critical that those providing leadership take care to structure processes and procedures for the selection or election of persons for leadership who understand and support that purpose and vision.

Such processes need to be open, fair, and redemptive, but clear criteria are needed for nomination and selection that include support of the congregation's purpose and vision. It is helpful to understand something about the different types of decision-making coalitions that can be found in congregations.

As illustrated in figure 6, there are different types of decision-making coalitions. All of them illustrate that there are both formal and informal leaders who influence the decisions that are made. A *narrow and concentrated* coalition, one that is often made up of a few extended families in a congregation, can lead to a congregation functioning more as a family system than as a congregation of the living Christ. A *broad and diffused* coalition is often found in congregations that have not attended to clarifying their purpose and vision. This can lead to indecision or even different groups vying to give direction to the congregation. A *multi-centered competitive* coalition means that there is conflict present in a congregation, whether it is still latent or whether it has already become manifest. Evidence of such coalitions being in place can be found when there is an active rumor mill at work or if there are groups of persons who have cut off communication with one another. A *center-representative* coalition is where those serving in formal roles of leadership, along with many of the informal persons of influence within the congregation, share some common understanding of and commitment to the congregation's purpose and vision.

Building capacity for ministry. Another component of congregational faithfulness and effectiveness is the ability to build capacity for ministry. In many ways, this is reflective of a biblical and theological understanding of stewardship. Congregations want to be wise stewards of the limited resources they have. Introducing change by first building capacity for making the change viable is not just good organizational thinking from an open systems perspective, it is also wise stewardship from a biblical and theological perspective. The most valuable resource that a congregation has available is its people. People bring with them their time, their goodwill, their gifts, skills, and abilities, and their financial resources. Learning to steward the

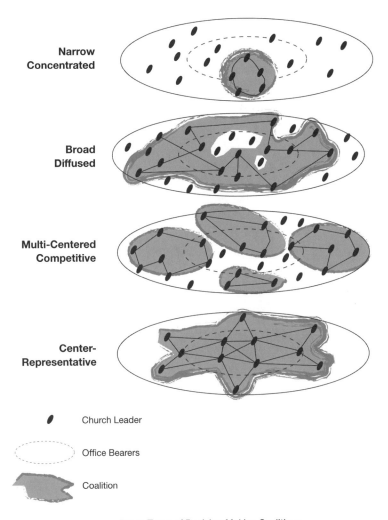

Narrow
Concentrated

Broad
Diffused

Multi-Centered
Competitive

Center-
Representative

🌢 Church Leader

⬯ Office Bearers

▰ Coalition

Fig. 6. Types of Decision-Making Coalitions

use of people in the course of building capacity for congregational ministry is essential for those who seek to provide faithful and effective leadership of congregations.

Commitment to continuous improvement. Congregations seeking to live into the redemptive reign of God in Christ are always searching for ways to improve what they are doing in stewarding the resources that are available. They are not satisfied with the status quo just because that's the way things are. They are interested in always asking the question, Is this the best way to be faithful and effective in what we are seeking to do? Often congregations find it useful to examine what others are doing in this area of ministry. Notions of benchmarking developed within the organizational literature come into play at this point. Congregations do not always have to reinvent the wheel, although, as pointed out in chapter 3, they must always attend to making sure that what they are learning from others is applied contextually to their ministry.

Attending to organizational culture. This is related to some of the other dimensions of congregational faithfulness and effectiveness that have been discussed, but it is helpful to name it as a separate dimension. Those seeking to provide leadership in congregations need to be able to "get on the balcony" as authors Ronald Heifetz and Marty Linsky would say.[3] They need to step back from time to time and get the bigger picture in view by attending to the life of the congregation as a whole or what can be labeled as the "organizational culture." This is manifest in such dimensions as the quality of relationships, overall atmosphere, and the element of trust that can be found in the congregation. Biblically and theologically, this has to do with seeking to be led by the Spirit. It is the Spirit's leadership in the life of a congregation that brings about the faithful exercise of the spiritual fruit and the effective exercise of the spiritual gifts. Attending to the organizational culture is an important way of discerning if there is something fundamentally wrong in the life of a congregation.

Guiding a Planned Change Process in a Congregation

Every congregation, as acknowledged in chapter 3, has to deal with the reality of change. Change is a constant. It is helpful in thinking about change in relationship to congregations to develop some understanding of how to guide a change process. Here we are dealing primarily with the concept of planned change, where specific changes are introduced by those seeking to provide leadership in congregations. Many of these ideas, however, are also helpful for dealing with unanticipated change. In this regard, it is important to remind ourselves that the ministry of the Spirit is as much about responding to conflict, disruption, interruption, and surprise as it is

166

about planning and strategy. This section deals primarily with change in terms of planning and strategy.

Planned change is important to understand because it provides an opportunity to exercise leadership for initiating new ideas and introducing new approaches to ministry. Leadership can be more responsive to taking such initiative if it makes careful use of the evaluation and feedback processes that are available from an open systems perspective. In a congregation, some of this evaluation and feedback has to do with collecting data (wisdom and planning) while some of it also has to do with engaging in discernment of how the Spirit may be leading (faith and discernment).

The field of planned change can be accessed by congregation leaders to provide them with a set of conceptual frameworks and processes to assist in the activity of introducing new initiatives. Three of these conceptual frameworks are introduced below: types of planned change, a process of going through a planned change, and typical responses to planned change.

Types of Planned Change

Not all changes introduced into a congregation have the same level of complexity or difficulty associated with them, and not all elicit the same level of resistance. Adding a part-time staff member for youth ministry, for example, is usually less complex and encounters less resistance in most congregations than trying to transition a more traditional style of worship service into a seeker-friendly format that uses a different style of music. The first type of change, in these examples, represents adding something new, which was not present before, while the second involves a congregation having to unlearn one way of engaging in worship while relearning a whole new approach in terms of style. These different levels of complexity are directly related to different levels of resistance to change. More complex changes typically encounter higher levels of resistance. This relationship is displayed in figure 7, which also displays the four types of planned change that can be utilized.[4]

Complexity or difficulty—first and second order changes. The horizontal axis represents the level of complexity or difficulty that a particular change introduces into the life of a congregation. The basic idea is

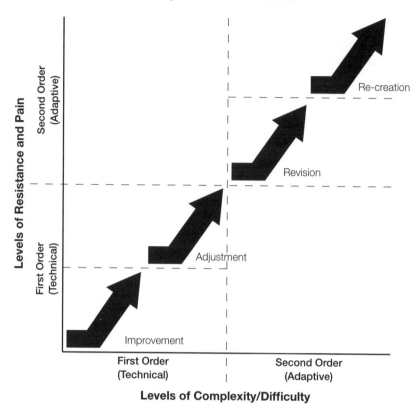

Fig. 7. Types of Planned Change

that different changes have different levels of complexity or difficulty associated with them. Persons seeking to provide leadership in a congregation are well served by being aware of what level of complexity is most likely involved in a particular change that is being introduced.

This variation in complexity and difficulty is conceptualized around first order and second order levels of change—what Heifetz and Linsky refer to as technical and adaptive types of change.[5] First order changes are those that take place within the current values and assumptions that people hold about the life of a congregation. In such changes, what might be called the "fundamental rules of congregational life" are not being changed. When one encounters a second order change, some of the core values or core beliefs are being redefined. This is why second order changes usually invoke higher levels of resistance and introduce higher levels of pain in a congregation.

Resistance and pain—first order and second order. The vertical axis represents the level of resistance and pain that a congregation will encounter when any planned change is introduced. Every change will elicit at least some resistance in a congregation. As changes become more complex and move into the area of being second order, it is understandable that there will be higher levels of resistance and pain that are encountered.

What is important to note is that encountering resistance and pain is not necessarily to be seen as a problem. Often the *background noise* that it generates is part of the process of people coming to terms with the change that is taking place. While resistance can manifest itself as problematic behavior if people start behaving in unhelpful ways, those providing leadership need to be careful not to overreact in such cases. Creating space for people to be able to voice their concerns and express their feelings is part of the dynamics of going through the change process. There will always be at least some uneasiness in a congregation when it faces something new. A grieving process is often required to help people work through the process of becoming familiar with the new and letting go of the old. For some this is more difficult than for others.

Those seeking to provide leadership in a congregation need to discern the level of complexity of the changes they want to introduce and also anticipate the level of resistance that will likely be encountered. In doing so, they will be better able to interpret what is happening when the life of a congregation becomes disrupted. They will also be better able to utilize the strategies available as they help people work through the dynamics of the change process.

Understanding the Four Types of Change

It is helpful to understand the various types of planned change that can be introduced into the life of a congregation. Understanding these types in relationship to complexity and resistance provides a useful framework for designing a given intervention as well as for helping to guide the process once it is set in motion.

Improvement. There are two ways that a congregation can introduce an improvement. The first, as illustrated above with the addition of the part-time youth minister, represents a new initiative where something is being added to the present ministry that was not there before. The second way to make an improvement is to upgrade an aspect of the ministry, such as replacing an inadequate sound system with new equipment. These planned changes do not fundamentally challenge the core values or beliefs of a congregation. While they may encounter some resistance and introduce some pain, these can usually be dealt with in fairly simple ways—practicing good communication, meeting with a few key people or groups, or inviting feedback and suggestions.

Adjustment. An adjustment is a type of planned change that adds another dimension to the process. In this case, a congregation is required to unlearn the way it has been doing something and to relearn a new way to do it. Such changes are more difficult to make and typically elicit higher levels of resistance. An example of an adjustment would be a congregation that finds its worship seating overly crowded and decides that it needs to go to two services. This decision requires two phases of response from the congregation. First, persons have to let go of their familiar way of being together for worship (e.g., one set time where everyone is present). Second, they need to adjust to a new set of choices for being in worship (e.g., choose between two times for worship and accept not seeing everyone at the service they attend). In addition, an adjustment like this usually introduces other changes into the congregation as a system, such as having to decide whether to have one church school period or two, having to staff two services with greeters, ushers, musicians, and having staff time used in leading two services.

While the underlying values and beliefs are not being challenged with this type of adjustment, as long as the two services are basically duplicates of one another in style, the disruption to the life of the congregation is more substantial. There are typically higher levels of resistance elicited along with more pain being expressed. Such changes usually require more time to become accepted and institutionalized and also require more time and energy to process on the part of those providing leadership.

Improvements and adjustments represent first order, planned changes. These changes typically can be introduced without making any fundamental changes in a congregation's vision for ministry or its core values and beliefs. People simply have to get used to new or

170

improved ways of doing things, or relearn some new ways of engaging in familiar behaviors. It is when the next level of planned change is encountered that we enter into second order change.

Revision. When a change is introduced that requires a redirection of a congregation's ministry or a reorientation of the basic vision of a congregation, then a congregation is encountering a revisioning type of change. Here something in the core identity of the church is being shifted, or some of the core values and beliefs are being challenged and changed. To follow on the previous example, assume that a congregation going to a two-service worship format decides to make the two services different in style. One maintains the more traditional style, while the other adopts a seeker-friendly format with a different style of music. Given time, people will typically begin to raise questions about whether the congregation is becoming two congregations and will begin to debate what really represents biblically and theologically sound worship. They sense that something fundamental in the identity, values, or beliefs of the congregation is shifting or has changed. And they are correct—a second order change is taking place in the congregation.

What is critical for those seeking to provide leadership in a congregation is to anticipate the resistance which will be encountered and to provide intentional ways for this to be engaged. This might include (a) extensive conversation with key leaders and groups in the congregation most affected by the change before the change is introduced, (b) regular opportunities for feedback through focus groups and public forums, and (c) communication offering a clear articulation of why the change is being made that provides a biblical and theological rationale for it.

Re-creation. There are times when a congregation is facing the challenge of having to fundamentally reinvent itself in order to survive. The way that it has functioned in terms of its core identity and values is obsolete. This type of change is what is known as a re-creation. An example would be a congregation that has encountered a major transition in the racial-ethnic makeup of the population in its context. Given time, such congregations are usually faced with having to serve and reach a very different group of persons in order to survive in their present location. A change of this magnitude is very complex, and a congregation facing such a change will typically experience

171

very high levels of resistance and extensive expressions of pain if it pursues re-creation.

The process of re-creating is complicated for many congregations because they often resist changing until it is too late. Usually there is a time lag of years between re-creation being required and when those providing leadership in a congregation are able to come to grips with it. By the time they come to terms with what is required to re-create, they have lost the opportunity to do so. As they delay, many of the more visionary members usually have left due to inaction in the congregation, and financial resources have declined. In this situation, many congregations often relocate in order to preserve their current identity and core values. Very few congregations have been able to go through a successful re-creation.

Planned changes that involve revisioning or re-creation represent second order changes. Today, most congregations are facing at least the challenge of revisioning. Persons providing leadership in congregations need to realize the importance of discerning where a congregation is in terms of engaging its context in ministry in meaningful ways.

Applying the four types of change. Each type of change in this framework needs to be understood as being distinct and basically self-contained. This means that each type of change is discrete and has its own logic. Just multiplying strategies around one type will not take you to the next level. The most important point in this pattern is to be aware of the shift that takes place between first order and second order types of change. Increasing the number of improvements and adjustments will not be sufficient to bring a congregation through a revisioning process, even though it might create some capacity for doing so.

The Cycle Encountered in the Process of Change

Every planned change introduced into a congregation will go through a process of gradually being accepted and institutionalized. This process typically has some distinct phases associated with it, especially when it involves second order changes of revisioning and re-creation. It is important for those seeking to provide Spirit-led leadership in congregations to be familiar with the dynamics of this process of how a congregation comes to accept change.

172

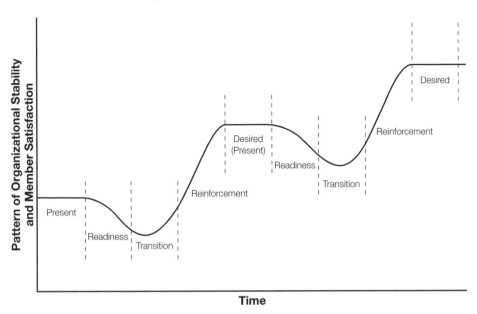

Fig. 8. The Cycle of the Process of Change

As illustrated in figure 8, the typical process of change, especially second order change, goes through five phases. These take place within the congregation over an extended period of time.[6]

Time. The variable of time is represented on the horizontal axis. Changes take place over time. The length of time for a change will vary, related usually to its level of complexity and difficulty. What is important to understand for those providing leadership is to develop a planning window for introducing a change that is realistic and consistent with the type of change being introduced. Planned changes that are rushed or those which are extended over too long a period of time can often generate unnecessary conflict or lose their effectiveness.

Congregational stability and member satisfaction. The vertical axis represents the sense of congregational stability and member satisfaction with what is going on in the life of the congregation. The basic premise is that a planned change that is introduced into a congregation will tend to destabilize, at least for a time, the sense of the "way things are" and be perceived as being "disruptive." This will typically result in a loss of a sense of stability in the congregation

173

and will manifest some level of dissatisfaction from members with what is happening.

What is important to understand is that the sense of congregational stability and member satisfaction will typically go down for a period of time. This is *normal* behavior that persons providing leadership need to understand. If they fail to understand this, they may be tempted to withdraw a planned change prematurely, just because it is generating some dissatisfaction, and attempt to return to the status quo. Doing so can generate other problems, as illustrated in the welcoming newcomers/handshake example that opened this chapter—the leadership gave away its power to a vocal minority and with it gave away making any other changes in regard to that issue for at least another decade.

When people are dissatisfied with something, they express their resistance and pain in different ways. There is always some background noise when changes are made. Those providing Spirit-led leadership must learn to listen to dissatisfied persons with compassion but also with discernment. It is important not to necessarily equate volume of complaints with number of complaints. It is also important for those who lead to be intentional in providing ways for persons to express their concerns and dissatisfaction in helpful ways by structuring public opportunities to do so (e.g., convening a focus group, implementing a survey, or conducting a town meeting with open-mike opportunities).

Five Phases in the Change Cycle

As noted above and in figure 8, the typical planned change intervention goes through five phases. It is important for those providing Spirit-led leadership to understand the dynamics of each phase, if they want to help guide the change process in ways that encourage them to respond more redemptively to resistance and member dissatisfaction.

Present state. The present state is a general acceptance of *the way things are*. Even though there may be an issue that needs to be addressed, it has not yet been adequately recognized or named as an issue, at least not officially, by those in leadership. While there may be a few voices or groups within a congregation that are expressing concern about something, no action has been taken to do anything about this matter.

An example of the present state phase is a congregation whose worship center has a seating capacity of 550 and an average worship attendance of over 500 in its one service. Typically on holidays and for special services, overflow seating needs to be arranged. Such a congregation is way past being visitor-friendly in terms of welcoming guests into its service, but for the most part members usually accept the crowding. While some may be frustrated that they can't get their normal seat on some Sundays or some may raise objections to having to use an overflow room on special Sundays, for the most part people accept the status quo as the way things are.

Readiness. The congregation enters into the readiness phase of the change process when the issue comes to the attention of those involved in the decision-making process of the congregation. The issue has now been named publicly and, therefore, expectations begin to be generated that something needs to be done. Typical characteristics of this phase are:

- public discussion begins to take place among the leaders regarding what the issue is and what might be done
- discomfort increases as more information surfaces
- discussion begins about possible alternative solutions
- dissatisfaction increases as persons express their concerns with the issue or their concerns with proposed alternative solutions

In the example suggested above, the church council might form a special task force to study the problem and to make recommendations. With such a move, the issue now is both public and official, and it invites discussion among the members, whether solicited or not. Congregational stability and member satisfaction begin to go down as people discuss and debate alternative solutions—e.g., should we add on to the facility, should we go to two services, should we plant a daughter congregation, and so on. Some persons may even organize in order to try to shape the decision process or to force an early decision. Usually, those who like things the way they are will begin to become defensive and resistant to the discussion of any change being necessary.

It is important for leaders to understand that when no decision has yet been made, the congregation's sense of stability and member satisfaction are going to go down. The reason this happens is because the message was sent that a problem is being studied, which is also a message that a decision is going to be made and that, likely, a change will be forthcoming. This is part of the process of change. It is not uncommon during this phase for some persons to organize themselves to lobby for a particular change. It is important during this phase to find constructive ways to invite input into the process of study and evaluation. Properly guided, this phase of destabilization can be a helpful preparation for the change that will eventually be introduced.

Transition. The phase of transition occurs when a congregation makes a specific decision about how to address the issue that has been named. It should be noted that even a decision to do nothing introduces a change into the congregation, because expectations have been set in motion. Usually, if an issue is a serious one that needs to be addressed, a decision will be made to introduce a planned change. Implementing such a decision is the point in the process where a congregation usually experiences the most instability and dissatisfaction. Spirit-led leaders must understand that this is a normal part of the process of change, lest they attempt to resolve such disruption by trying to go back to the way things were, which is not possible at this point. Typical characteristics of this phase are:

- a sense of loss of control among those who are in leadership
- expressions of anxiety about the future or fear about what is happening
- significant expressions of resistance or pain from some persons or groups

To continue the example above, the congregation's council may have made a decision to go to a two-service format for Sunday morning worship, with one of the two services also changing its format to a seeker-friendly style. The rationale they might provide is that they are doing this to create more space for visitors as well as more bridges to connect with different people. The theological foundation they might provide is that they want to reach a more diverse cross-section of people and be able to show hospitality to those who are guests. Everyone is affected. Everyone has to make choices, such as which service to attend in terms of time and relative to preferred style.

It is not uncommon at this point in the process of change for a group to form as the loyal opposition who oppose the change that's being made and engage in holding special meetings. Some may even threaten to leave or to withhold their giving if the congregation insists on going this direction. Others may begin to publicly criticize the leaders, challenging their decisions and attempting to undermine their authority. While the level of resistance and dissatisfaction may vary from issue to issue, one thing is certain: congregational stability and member satisfaction continue to go down for a time as the change is introduced.

This is the point where leaders responsible for introducing the change may be tempted to withdraw the proposal and attempt to return to the previous status quo. But it is too late. The disruption that has been set in motion includes expectations toward making the change. There is no going back. In proceeding to implement the change that was introduced, typically there is a point where things begin to stabilize a bit and member dissatisfaction begins to quiet down, although it does not yet go away. This is the point where persons are beginning to reconcile themselves to the change and get used to it. Some begin to adopt the change as their own, while others at least begin to come to terms with the change being the new reality.

Reinforcement. As a planned change begins to take hold in the life of a congregation, there is typically more of a sense of congregational stability and member satisfaction. Critical at this phase of the process is for Spirit-led leaders to find ways to reinforce the change that has been introduced. There are a variety of ways they can do this:

- solicit feedback from persons through surveys on ways to improve the implementation process
- conduct pulse groups and public forums to invite ways to improve the implementation process
- provide information on what is happening because of the change (e.g., report on the number of total persons attending worship as this begins to go up)

- spend time with those who were disaffected by the change to listen to their concerns, without giving in to their demands

Often what happens in a situation like this is that persons will at first tolerate a change when it is introduced but over time gradually come to terms with it. Many people have to live into a change to understand what it was about. It is not uncommon that some who were early critics of the proposed change even become active supporters of it once they have lived through it and begun to experience it. A critical part of the reinforcement phase is to recognize that initial acceptance does not constitute institutionalization. Second order changes often take many months, and possibly several years, to become widely accepted and supported. It is important in those congregations that rotate their elected leaders to insure that commitments to the changes that were made are part of the criteria for the election or selection of new leaders.

Desired state. The final phase of the change cycle occurs when the change has come to be accepted as part of a new understanding of *the way things are.* This represents the preferred state and typically displays the following characteristics:

- a feedback process is established to continue to measure progress associated with the change that was made
- new problems associated with the change that was made have been identified and addressed
- the preferred state has become part of the accepted vision of the congregation
- a coalition of leaders supports the change and makes sure that it stays in place
- the background noise has settled down to a low whisper, if still present

There are two dynamics related to the preferred state to which leaders need to attend. First, the preferred state should show increased levels of support from among persons in terms of their satisfaction. The extent to which this occurs is usually related to the effectiveness of the process that was guided by the leaders. If disaffected people were handled well during the process or if communication was regular and two-way, then typically a congregation will experience a higher level of support for the change long term.

Second, the preferred state is never static. A congregation never "arrives" in the course of being guided through the change process. Usually there are new issues facing a congregation as a result of the change that was introduced. To extend the example used above, the congregation that goes to two services to increase space for more to attend worship typically finds its educational program overwhelmed with more children and adults. This may create space problems inside the building as well as have implications for parking. Having to decide whether to build for more space or run a double church school program that matches the two worship services represents new issues that need to be addressed.

Planned change is typically a process that is ongoing. For a congregation that is being led by the Spirit to engage its context with meaningful ministry, the process of guiding change is usually a continuous responsibility of those who provide leadership for a congregation.

Types of Responses to Change

One of the more interesting aspects of guiding the change process is for leaders to be aware that persons' responses to the process vary when it is introduced. The planned change literature indicates that there is a discernible pattern of such responses. This is displayed in figure 9, where the six responses to change are noted.[7] While this figure is drawn as a perfect bell curve, the reality is that the curve can bulge either way in different congregations. New congregations often have more persons in the categories on the left of the curve, while those in established congregations that have strong traditions often have more persons on the right of the curve. It should also be noted that, depending on the issue to be addressed, persons might find themselves at any of the five possible response patterns. While they may tend to have a basic pattern, this pattern may not always be their first response.

Innovators. These persons are usually a small percentage of a congregation, but represent a key source for generating new ideas. Innovators tend to thrive on change and tend not to like the status

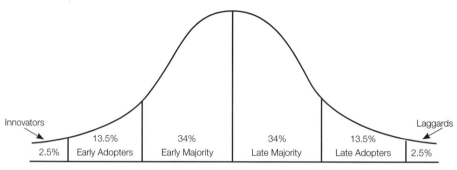

Fig. 9. Persons' Responses to Change. Reprinted and adapted from
Everett M. Rogers, *Diffusion of Innovations*, 5th ed. (New York: Free Press, 2003).

quo. They are usually looking for new ways to do things and can quickly adjust their thinking and behavior to support new ideas. It is not uncommon for such persons to come up with many more ideas than a typical congregation can, or needs to, implement at any one time. Because of this, innovators often feel misunderstood and underappreciated by the majority of persons in the congregation. It is important to provide innovators with an opportunity to have a voice, but it is also important to make sure they understand the limits of how much change is needed, or viable, at any given point.

Early adopters. A larger group in the typical congregation is made up of persons who tend to be change oriented but who do not necessarily come up with the new ideas. These are the early adopters, persons who can read or hear a proposal for change and see it as already being a reality. The logic and rationale for a proposal is sufficient for them to accept the proposed change. These persons are key figures for helping to visualize what a change might look like and how to anticipate its implementation. It is important for congregational leaders to cultivate the support of early adopters in pursuing a change strategy. These persons can often help to sell an idea to others. But it is also important for congregational leaders to recognize when too many innovators and early adopters may be involved in the decision process for making changes, lest they get too far ahead of guiding the process in the congregation.

Early majority and late majority. As noted earlier, many persons have to live through a change in order to understand it and begin to appreciate it. This reflects the fact that many persons in congregations, and the population at large, are part of the early or late majority. They represent the broad segment of middle adopters. They are not necessarily opposed to a change, although they may express some early resistance. It is usually only after they have experienced it that it makes sense to them. Persons in the early majority take time to deliberate new ideas yet tend to adopt them just before the average person would. Persons in the late majority consider peer decisions more directly and tend to adopt new ideas after the average persons would. This is why the pattern of congregational stability and member satisfaction often continue to go down during the readiness and transition phases of the change process. This is also why it is so important for congregational leaders to keep perspective during these phases and to realize that things will usually begin to settle down as people begin to live into the change.

Late adopters. Another response to change comes from those who might be called late adopters. Sometimes these persons will actively resist the change for some time before coming to accept the reality of it. These are persons who may continue to not appreciate the change that was made, but have come to accept that this is the way things are going to be. Persons with this response can often create significant discomfort in the congregation during the change cycle all the way up to and through the reinforcement phase. Church leaders need to be alert to structuring opportunities for such persons to be heard. They also need to recognize that it is likely that such persons will not fundamentally modify their opinion about the change, even if they come to accept it as the new reality.

Laggards. Not untypically, there is often a small number of persons in a congregation who will continue to resist and even challenge the change. It is also not uncommon for such persons to seek to generate support from among others to join them in fighting against the change that was made. Some of these persons may function out of principle, and it is important for the leadership to listen carefully to them in trying to discern their concerns and their issues. But others may turn the situation into a power confrontation and create unhealthy disruption. It is also not uncommon for some of these persons to utilize spiritual language, such as being "led by the Lord," in waging their campaign. These persons can represent a real challenge to the leaders of a congregation. While leaders need to be very careful not to label someone too quickly as a laggard, they also ought not be naïve about the reality that such a disposition can be the case for some persons. Usually laggards will attempt to generate conflict to get their way. At this point, Spirit-led leaders of a congregation need to understand the difference between guiding change and addressing conflict.

Let the Church Be the Church

This book has attempted to make the case that the challenge facing the church in the U.S. today is not primarily a crisis in understanding its purpose or in defining strategies for its ministry, although these have their place. Rather, the challenge is one of living into all that the Triune God intends the church to be in light of its creation by the Spirit. The church created by the Spirit is missionary by nature—it is called, gathered, and sent into the world to participate fully in God's mission. It is crucial for a congregation to understand its missionary nature if it is to live into all that God intends. A congregation being led by the Spirit is the foundation for this understanding and the ministry that results from it. The call of this book is simply this: let the church be the church—a Spirit-led, missional church that seeks to participate fully in God's mission in its particular context.

Notes

Chapter 1 Spirit-Led Ministry

1. Each of the illustrations used in this book represents actual experiences that I have encountered in working with churches, though some of them are composites of source materials from several congregations. Names and places have been changed in all cases.

2. See, for example, the use of this approach by Rick Warren, *Purpose Driven Church* (Grand Rapids: Zondervan, 1995).

3. See, for example, the development of this approach by George G. Hunter III, *Church for the Unchurched* (Nashville: Abingdon, 1996).

4. See, for example, the development of this approach by Dan Kimball, *The Emerging Church* (Grand Rapids: Zondervan, 2003).

5. Darrell L. Guder, ed., *Missional Church: A Vision for the Sending of the Church in North America* (Grand Rapids: Eerdmans, 1998).

6. See, for example, Darrell L. Guder, *The Continuing Conversation of the Church* (Grand Rapids: Eerdmans, 2000); Craig Van Gelder, *The Essence of the Church: A Community Created by the Spirit* (Grand Rapids: Baker, 2000); and Richard H. Bliese and Craig Van Gelder, *The Evangelizing Church: A Lutheran Contribution* (Minneapolis: Augsburg Fortress, 2005).

7. Lois Barrett, ed., *Treasure in Clay Jars: Patterns of Missional Faithfulness* (Grand Rapids: Eerdmans, 2004).

8. Van Gelder, *Essence of the Church*, 157.

9. It was the 1952 meeting of the International Missionary Council (IMC) in Willingen, Germany that began to shift the thinking about mission from the church having a mission, to God being a missionary God with a mission in which the church participated. This was based on conceiving of mission from a fuller trinitarian perspective rather than trying to ground the work of the church primarily on a Christology. Following that meeting of the IMC this understanding became known as the *missio Dei*. Further explanation of the theological perspective that informs the *missio Dei* may be found in chapter 5.

10. Van Gelder, *Essence of the Church*, 74–76.

11. See Lesslie Newbigin, *The Open Secret: An Introduction to the Theology of Mission*, rev. ed. (Grand Rapids: Eerdmans, 1995).

Chapter 2 Spirit-Led Ministry in the Bible

1. Michael Welker, *God the Spirit*, trans. John F. Hoffmeyer (Minneapolis: Fortress, 1994), x.

2. A helpful summary of this argument is developed in Lesslie Newbigin, *Foolishness to the Greeks: The Gospel and Western Culture* (Grand Rapids: Eerdmans, 1986).

3. See, for example, J. Richard Middleton and Brian J. Walsh, *Truth Is Stranger Than It Used to Be: Biblical Faith in a Postmodern Age* (Downers Grove, IL: InterVarsity, 1995).

4. Van Gelder, *Essence of the Church*, 88–90.

5. Ibid., 90–93.

6. Welker, *God the Spirit*, 142.

7. Ibid., 3–5.

8. This summary list of dimensions draws substantially from many of the insights developed by Michael Welker, but represents this author's framing of the categories.

9. Welker, *God the Spirit*, 58.

10. Other passages of Scripture reference this as the public installation of Jesus for the ministry that God intended (e.g., Rom. 1:4; Heb. 9:14).

11. Welker, *God the Spirit*, 228.

Chapter 3 Spirit-Led Ministry in Context

1. David A. Nadler, Robert B. Shaw, A. Elise Walton, and Associates, *Discontinuous Change: Leading Organizational Transformation* (San Francisco: Jossey-Bass, 1995).

2. Craig Van Gelder, "Missional Context: Understanding North American Culture," in Darrell L. Guder, ed., *Missional Church: A Vision for the Sending of the Church in North America* (Grand Rapids: Eerdmans, 1998), 18–45.

3. A helpful introduction to this concept is found in Charles Trueheart, "Welcome to the Next Church," *Atlantic Monthly* 278, no. 2 (August 1996): 37–58.

4. See Barry Johnson, *Polarity Management: Identifying and Managing Unsolvable Problems* (Amherst, MA: HRD Press, 1992).

5. This point is ably argued by Lesslie Newbigin, *The Gospel in a Pluralist Society* (Grand Rapids: Eerdmans, 1989); see esp. 80–115.

6. The concept of "translatability" is used here to describe the way in which the message of the gospel comes to expression within a specific culture, where it becomes embedded in and is expressed in relation to the language, worldview, and customs of that context. A helpful resource in understanding this point is Lamin Sanneh, *Translating the Message: The Missionary Impact on Culture* (Maryknoll, NY: Orbis Books, 2002).

7. This point is developed by Van Gelder, *Essence of the Church*, 118–20.

8. See Nancy T. Ammerman, *Congregation and Community* (New Brunswick, NJ: Rutgers University Press, 1997); Nancy T. Ammerman, Jackson W. Carroll, Carl S. Dudley, William McKinney, eds., *Studying Congregations: A New Handbook* (Nashville: Abingdon, 1998); Dorothy C. Bass, ed., *Practicing Our Faith: A Way of Life for a Searching People* (San Francisco: Jossey-Bass, 1997); Jackson W. Carroll, Carl S. Dudley, and William McKinney, *Handbook for Congregational Studies* (Nashville: Abingdon, 1986); and Carl S. Dudley and Nancy T. Ammerman, *Congregations in Transition: A Guide for Analyzing, Assessing, and Adapting in Changing Communities* (San Francisco : Jossey-Bass, 2002).

9. Andrew F. Walls, *The Missionary Movement in Christian History: Studies in the Transmission of Faith* (Maryknoll, NY: Orbis Books, 1996).

10. Sanneh, *Translating the Message*.

Chapter 4 Spirit-Led Ministry in the U.S. Context and in the Missional Church

1. This chapter is adapted from an article first published as "From Corporate Church to Missional Church: The Challenge Facing Congregations Today," *Review and Expositor* 101, no. 3 (Summer 2004): 425–50.

2. Van Gelder, *Essence of the Church*, 120–22.

3. The Willow Creek website offers the following description. "Since 1992, the Willow Creek Association has been linking like-minded, action-oriented churches with each other and with strategic vision, training, and resources. Our desire is to serve local church leaders in building biblically functioning churches that reach increasing numbers of lost people, not just with innovations from Willow Creek, but with God-given breakthroughs with widespread potential from any church in the world. The WCA is a not-for-profit ministry with more than 11,000 Member Churches from 90 denominations and 45 countries. They represent a wide variety of sizes, denominations and backgrounds, and are ministering in literally every corner of the world." http://www.willowcreek.com/wca_info/ (accessed March 25, 2007).

4. R. Daniel Reeves and Ronald Jenson, *Always Advancing: Modern Strategies for Church Growth* (San Bernardino, CA: Here's Life Publishers, 1984), 91–136.

5. Sidney E. Mead, "Denominationalism: The Shape of Protestantism in America," in Russell E. Richey, ed., *Denominationalism* (Nashville: Abingdon, 1977), 71.

6. Clearly there are different understandings regarding the rationale for the established church among Roman Catholics, Orthodox, Lutherans, and Calvinists, but common to all is the core understanding that the established church represents the primary location of God's activity in that particular geographical location since the boundaries of the church's domain are the same as the boundaries of the world that it possesses. For the specifics regarding the differences among established church views, a helpful treatment is provided by Ernst Troeltsch, *The Social Teaching of the Christian Churches, Volume II* (1912; repr., Louisville: Westminster/John Knox, 1992).

7. An example of this perspective is found in the Westminster Confession of Faith (1646) in chapter 25, "Of the Church," where one reads in section 2, "The visible Church . . . is the Kingdom of the Lord Jesus Christ. . . ." This connecting of Jesus's announcement of the kingdom (see footnote references in the confession to this section) makes the visible church and God's kingdom on earth the same entity. John H. Leith, *Creeds of the Church: A Reader in Christian Doctrine From the Bible to the Present* (Richmond: John Knox Press, 1973), 192–229.

8. The Peace of Augsburg in 1555 established this principle, but it was not until the end of the religious Thirty Years' War (1618–1648) and the Peace of Westphalia in 1648 that this principle became the accepted practice. See Eric W. Gritsch, *A History of Lutheranism* (Minneapolis: Fortress, 2002), 109–13.

9. Troeltsch, *Social Teaching of the Christian Churches*, 461–94, 671–73, 691–94.

10. These five phases are introduced as a framework for understanding denominations by Russell E. Richey's article "Denominations and Denominationalism: An American Morphology," in Robert Bruce Mullin and Russell E. Richey, eds., *Reimagining Denominationalism: Interpretive Essays* (New York: Oxford University Press, 1994), 77–90.

11. Sydney E. Ahlstrom, *A Religious History of the American People* (New Haven: Yale University Press, 1972), 146–50.

12. John Corrigan and Winthrop S. Hudson, *Religion in America*, 7th ed. (Upper Saddle River, NJ: Pearson/Prentice Hall, 2004), 47–48.

13. Corrigan and Hudson, *Religion in America*, 51–52; Ahlstrom, *Religious History of the American People*, 184–99.

14. Ahlstrom, *Religious History of the American People*, 151–65.

15. Corrigan and Hudson, *Religion in America*, 62–63; Ahlstrom, *Religious History of the American People*, 200–13.

16. See, for example, the Dordrecht Confession (1632) that was adopted by the Mennonites, especially article 8, "Of the Church of Christ." Leith, *Creeds of the Churches*, 292–308.

17. A helpful discussion of the shift to the gathered church as a voluntary organization in the midst of the breakdown of the parish system is provided by Corrigan and Hudson, *Religion in America*, 52.

18. Corrigan and Hudson, *Religion in America*, 52, 162–65.

19. Alexis de Tocqueville, *Democracy in America* (1835), as quoted by Ahlstrom, *Religious History of the American People*, 386. Tocqueville said, "Religion in America takes no direct part in the government of society, but nevertheless it must be regarded as the foremost of the political institutions of that country; for if it does not import a taste for freedom, it facilitates the use of free institutions."

20. William W. Sweet, *The Story of Religion in America* (1930; repr., Grand Rapids: Baker, 1975), 155–71.

21. Amendment I: "Congress shall make no law respecting an establishment of religion, or prohibiting the free exercise thereof; or abridging the freedom of speech, or of the press; or the right of the people peaceably to assemble, and to petition the government for a redress of grievances."

22. Corrigan and Hudson, *Religion in America*, 138–46, illustrates how this pattern was true for the Methodists in 1784, the Anglicans in 1785, and the Presbyterians in 1789.

23. Martin E. Marty, *Righteous Empire: The Protestant Experience in America* (New York: Dial Press, 1970), 67–68.

24. Richey, *Denominationalism*, 19–21.

25. Ahlstrom, *Religious History of the American People*, 96.

26. Mary Jo Hatch, *Organizational Theory: Modern, Symbolic, and Postmodern Perspectives* (New York: Oxford University Press, 1997), 119–22.

27. See Marty, *Righteous Empire*, 68; Corrigan and Hudson, *Religion in America*, 150–57; and Ahlstrom, *Religious History of the American People*, 429–54.

28. A helpful perspective on this conflict is provided by Elwyn A. Smith, "The Forming of a Modern American Denomination," in Richey, *Denominationalism*, 108–36 (see chap. 4, n. 5; cf. n. 24 above).

29. Corrigan and Hudson, *Religion in America*, 159–68.

30. See Smith, "Forming of a Modern American Denomination," 108–36.

31. William Carey proposed the formation of a mission society as the way to fund the work of missionaries. William Carey, *An Enquiry into the Obligation of Christians to Use Means for the Conversion of the Heathens* (1792; repr., London: Hodder and Stoughton, 1892), 82–83.

32. Corrigan and Hudson, *Religion in America*, 103–4; Ahlstrom, *Religious History of the American People*, 382–83.

33. For example, see the Presbyterians as discussed by Smith, "Forming of a Modern American Denomination," 108–36.

34. Fred J. Hood, "Evolution of the Denomination Among the Reformed in the Middle and Southern States, 1780–1840," in Richey, *Denominationalism*, 139–60.

35. Corrigan and Hudson, *Religion in America*, 246–54.

36. Ibid.; Ahlstrom, *Religious History of the American People*, 741–42.

37. Ahlstrom, *Religious History of the American People*, 858.

38. Russell E. Richey, "Denominations and Denominationalism: An American Morphology," in Mullin and Richey, *Reimagining Denominationalism*, 82–84.

39. Ibid., 84–87.

40. In the early decades of the twentieth century at least three streams emerged, which were Scientific Management by Frederick Taylor (1911), Administrative Management by Henri Fayol (1919), and Bureaucracy by Max Weber (1924).

41. Shailer Mathews, *Scientific Management in the Churches* (Chicago: The University of Chicago Press, 1912).

42. The dynamics of this new suburban growth are captured well by David Halberstam, *The Fifties* (New York: Villard Books, 1993), 131–43. In this section he discusses the beginning of mass-produced suburban housing as it was developed at Levittown, New York.

43. Ibid.

44. Gibson Winter, *The Suburban Captivity of the Churches: An Analysis of Protestant Responsibility in the Expanding Metropolis* (New York: Macmillan, 1962).

45. Ibid., 96–101.

46. Wade Clark Roof and William McKinney, *American Mainline Religion: Its Changing Shape and Future* (New Brunswick, NJ: Rutgers University Press, 1987), 48–57.

47. Lyle E. Schaller, *44 Questions for Church Planters* (Nashville: Abingdon, 1991), 13–36.

48. Roof and McKinney, *American Mainline Religion*.

49. Robert Wuthnow, *The Restructuring of American Religion* (Princeton, NJ: Princeton University Press, 1988).

50. The Evangelical Lutheran Church in America, newly formed in 1987, is a case study of the continuing pattern of denominational downsizing at the national level as revenues churchwide continue to decline. Most other mainline denominations follow a similar trend.

51. Roof and McKinney, *American Mainline Religion*, 152–55.

52. Ibid., 148–51.

53. Guder, *Missional Church*, 72–73.

54. Van Gelder, *Essence of the Church*, 20–21.

55. Warren, *Purpose Driven Church*.

56. See, for example, the recent book by Episcopal Bishop Claude E. Payne and Hamilton Beazley, *Reclaiming the Great Commission: A Practical Model for Transforming Denominations and Congregations* (San Francisco: Jossey-Bass, 2000).

57. See chapter 4, note 3.

58. The Emergent Village website offers the following description: "Emergent Village is a growing, generative friendship among missional Christians seeking to love our world in the Spirit of Jesus Christ. . . . By 2001, we had formed an organization around our friendship, known as Emergent, as a means of inviting more people into the conversation. Along with us, the 'emerging church' movement has been growing, and we in Emergent Village endeavor to fund the theological imaginations and spiritual lives of all who consider themselves a part of this broader movement." http://www.emergentvillage.org/about/ (accessed March 26, 2007).

59. A helpful summary of the wide variety of missiological and ecclesiological influences during this period is available in David J. Bosch, *Transforming Mission: Paradigm Shifts in Theology of Mission* (Maryknoll, NY: Orbis Books, 1991), 368–510.

60. Van Gelder, *Essence of the Church*, 31–44.

61. Bosch, *Transforming Mission*, 302–4.

62. It is interesting to note that many previous doctoral programs in missiology have now changed their nomenclature to *intercultural studies* in order to move past the appearance of Western imperialism that is often associated with the word *mission*.

63. Bosch, *Transforming Mission*, 389–93.

64. Johannes Blauw, *The Missionary Nature of the Church: A Survey of the Biblical Theology of Mission* (1962; repr., Grand Rapids: Eerdmans, 1974).

65. J. C. Hoekendijk, *The Church Inside Out* (Philadelphia: Westminster, 1964).

66. See especially the "Decree on the Church's Missionary Activity, Ad Gentes Divinitus," as available in Austin P. Flannery, ed., *Documents of Vatican II* (Grand Rapids: Eerdmans, 1975).

67. This convergence is helpfully discussed by James A. Scherer, *Gospel, Church and Kingdom: Comparative Studies in World Mission Theology* (Minneapolis: Augsburg, 1987).

68. Newbigin, *Open Secret*, 19–64.

69. See the Gospel and Our Culture Network website at www.gocn.org.

70. Guder, *Missional Church*.

71. Stanley J. Grenz, *The Social God and the Relational Self: A Trinitarian Theology of the Imago Dei* (Louisville: Westminster John Knox, 2001), 23–57.

72. John Zizioulas, *Being as Communion: Studies in Personhood and the Church* (Crestwood, NY: St. Vladimir's Seminary Press, 1985).

73. Miroslav Volf, *After Our Likeness: The Church as the Image of the Trinity* (Grand Rapids: Eerdmans, 1998).

74. This is the position argued by Van Gelder, *Essence of the Church*.

75. Some of the materials presented in this section are drawn from Craig Van Gelder, "For the Sake of the World," in Bliese and Van Gelder, *Evangelizing Church*.

76. Newbigin, *Gospel in a Pluralist Society*, 80–115.

Chapter 5 Spirit-Led Discernment and Decision Making

1. The substance of this chapter was first published under the title of "The Hermeneutics of Leading in Mission," in *Journal of Religious Leadership* 3, nos. 1–2 (2004):139–72.

2. This chapter uses the phrase "hermeneutical turn" as shorthand to explain the shift that occurred in human knowing during the twentieth century. This shift primarily involves the developments in philosophical hermeneutics, which have made us aware of the interpreted character of all human knowing, including the interpreted character of interpretation. For a fuller treatment of this hermeneutical turn, see Craig Van Gelder, "Method in Light of Scripture and in Relation to Hermeneutics," *Journal of Religious Leadership* 3, nos. 1–2 (Spring/Fall 2004): 43–73.

3. Jürgen Habermas, *The Theory of Communicative Action*, vols. 1–2, trans. Thomas McCarthy (Boston: Beacon Press, 1984, 1987).

4. The use of the word "God" here is intended to refer to a Christian confession of God as a Trinity—Father, Son, and Holy Spirit.

5. Edward Farley, *Theologia: The Fragmentation and Unity of Theological Education* (Philadelphia: Fortress, 1983). See also his later work, *The Fragility of Knowledge: Theological Education in the Church and the University* (Philadelphia: Fortress, 1988).

6. H. Richard Niebuhr, *The Purpose of the Church and Its Ministry* (New York: Harper & Row, 1956), 80–82.

7. Robert Banks, *Reenvisioning Theological Education: Exploring a Missional Alternative to Current Models* (Grand Rapids: Eerdmans, 1999).

8. Charles M. Wood, *Vision and Discernment: An Orientation in Theological Study* (Atlanta: Scholars Press, 1985).

9. Joseph C. Hough Jr. and John B. Cobb Jr., *Christian Identity and Theological Education* (Atlanta: Scholars Press, 1985).

10. The Mud Flower Collective, *God's Fierce Whimsy: Christian Feminism and Theological Education* (New York: Pilgrim Press, 1985).

11. Joseph C. Hough Jr. and Barbara G. Wheeler, *Beyond Clericalism: The Congregation as a Focus for Theological Education* (Atlanta: Scholars Press, 1988).

12. Rebecca S. Chopp, *Saving Work: Feminist Practices of Theological Education* (Louisville: Westminster John Knox, 1995).

13. Max L. Stackhouse, *Apologia: Contextualization, Globalization, and Mission in Theological Education* (Grand Rapids: Eerdmans, 1988).

14. David H. Kelsey, *To Understand God Truly: What's Theological about a Theological School* (Louisville: Westminster/John Knox, 1992); David H. Kelsey, *Between Athens and Berlin: The Theological Education Debate* (Grand Rapids: Eerdmans, 1993).

15. James D. Whitehead and Evelyn Eaton Whitehead, *Method in Ministry: Theological Reflection and Christian Ministry*, rev. ed. (Kansas City: Sheed & Ward, 1995).

16. Howard W. Stone and James O. Duke, *How to Think Theologically* (Minneapolis: Fortress, 1996).

17. Patricia O'Connell Killen and John de Beer, *The Art of Theological Reflection* (New York: Crossroad, 2000).

18. Robert J. Schreiter, *Constructing Local Theologies* (Maryknoll, NY: Orbis Books, 1985).

19. Ibid., 25–36.

20. Stephen B. Bevans, *Models of Contextual Theology: Faith and Cultures*, rev. ed. (Maryknoll, NY: Orbis Books, 2002). The original version published in 1992 had five models, but Bevans added a sixth in the 2002 edition by incorporating the Gospel and Our Culture approach as an alternative.

21. Sanneh, *Translating the Message*.

22. Newbigin, *Gospel in a Pluralist Society*, 72.

23. Bass, *Practicing Our Faith*.

24. Miroslav Volf and Dorothy C. Bass, eds., *Practicing Theology: Beliefs and Practices in Christian Life* (Grand Rapids: Eerdmans, 2002), 18.

25. Gerben Heitink, *Practical Theology: History, Theory, Action Domains*, trans. Reinder Bruinsma (Grand Rapids: Eerdmans, 1999), 92–95.

26. Peter Canisius, *Handbook on Pastoral Theology* (1591), as reported in Heitink, *Practical Theology*, 98.

27. Heitink, *Practical Theology*, 95–97.

28. Friedrich Schleiermacher, *Brief Outline on the Study of Theology*, trans. Terrence N. Tice (1811; 1830; repr., Richmond: John Knox, 1966).

29. Don S. Browning, *A Fundamental Practical Theology: Descriptive and Strategic Proposals* (Minneapolis: Fortress, 1996), 43.

30. Browning, *Fundamental Practical Theology*.

31. Ibid., 243.

32. Heitink, *Practical Theology*, 124–47.

33. Ibid., 163–66.

34. Ibid., 135–44.

35. The argument developed here draws from the work of Hans-Georg Gadamer, *Truth and Method*, ed. Garrett Barden and John Cumming (New York: Seabury Press, 1975), especially as Gadamer's idea of "prejudice" is developed and used by Heitink, *Practical Theology*, 184.

36. It is recognized that just stating that Scripture provides a normative role obviously does not resolve the problem of interpreting Scripture. But this is where the interpretive work of the historical Christian faith needs to be brought into dynamic conversation with the interpretive process. It is also where Christian leaders, following the exhortation of Scripture to be in relation with one another, need to be willing to stay at the table and engage the conversation in the midst of differences and disagreements.

37. It is important to make a distinction between Christian practices and strategic action. The former involves our shared experiences, whether intentionally designed or tacitly present, in which there is embedded both explicit and implicit theology. Strategic action, by contrast, involves an intentionality toward resolution of some issue or the implementation of some decision. To lead in mission, Christian leaders need to be deeply

informed by Christian practices while also developing capacity to make choices to implement strategic action.

38. It is recognized, however, that there are numerous other expressions of Christian communities that might also utilize such an approach.

39. Guder, *Missional Church*. See also Van Gelder, *Essence of the Church*.

40. See "Ad Gentes Divinitus," in *Documents of Vatican II*, 813–56; see also Hans Küng, *The Church*, trans. Ray and Rosaleen Ockenden (New York: Sheed & Ward, 1967).

41. See, for example, Blauw, *Missionary Nature of the Church*; Hoekendijk, *Church Inside Out*; and George W. Weber, *The Congregation in Mission: Emerging Structures for the Church in an Urban World* (Nashville: Abingdon, 1964).

42. See Newbigin, *Open Secret*; Bosch, *Transforming Mission*; Guder, *Missional Church*; and Van Gelder, *Essence of the Church*.

43. Van Gelder, *Essence of the Church*.

44. A good example of this is available in Ammerman et al., *Studying Congregations*, 78–104.

45. Ibid., 40–77.

46. The strong reliance on representation and democratic process found among many churches with Reformed polities stands in contrast to the strong leader and personality-shaped character of many churches with congregational polities. So also, the directness of debate and articulation of difference often found among congregations with a German or Dutch heritage stands in contrast to the nuanced and more egalitarian approach often found among Scandinavian congregations.

47. See especially John 13–16 but also note the role of the Spirit in the book of Acts and the teaching of Paul in Romans 5–8 and 1 Corinthians 2–3.

48. See, for example, Kenneth O. Gangel and Samuel L. Canine, *Communication and Conflict Management: In Churches and Christian Organizations* (Eugene, OR: Wipf & Stock, 2002).

49. Kenneth C. Haugk, *Antagonists in the Church: How to Identify and Deal with Destructive Conflict* (Minneapolis: Augsburg, 1988).

50. Heitink, *Practical Theology*, 133–35.

51. Habermas, *Theory of Communicative Action*. See also Heitink, *Practical Theology*, 135–37.

52. Gadamer, *Truth and Method*, 367–69; John B. Thompson, ed., *Paul Ricoeur: Hermeneutics and the Human Sciences* (Cambridge: Cambridge University Press, 1981), 132–49.

53. Engaging this task moves the discussion to one of apologetics. See, for example, "Reasonableness of Faith" in Diogenes Allen, *Christian Belief in a Postmodern World: The Full Wealth of Conviction* (Louisville: Westminster John Knox, 1989), 128–48; and "Reason, Revelation, and Experience" in Newbigin, *Gospel in a Pluralist Society*, 52–65.

54. James A. Scherer, *Gospel, Church, & Kingdom: Comparative Studies in World Mission Theology* (Minneapolis: Augsburg, 1987).

55. Paul Ricoeur, *From Text to Action: Essays in Hermeneutics, II*, trans. Kathleen Blamey and John B. Thompson (Evanston, IL: Northwestern University Press, 1991), 144–45.

56. See Abbas Tashakkori and Charles Teddlie, *Mixed Methodology: Combining Qualitative and Quantitative Approaches* (Thousand Oaks, CA: Sage Publications, 1998) and John W. Cresswell, *Research Design: Qualitative, Quantitative, and Mixed Methods Approaches*, 2nd ed. (Thousand Oaks, CA: Sage Publications, 2003).

57. Hatch, *Organizational Theory*, 63–100.

58. See, for example, the work of John P. Kotter, *Leading Change* (Boston: Harvard Business School Press, 1996), which is often referenced in the Christian literature on organizational change.

59. Heitink, *Practical Theology*, 148–77.

60. See Bass, *Practicing Our Faith*; and Volf and Bass, *Practicing Theology*.

61. One should note here the similarity in perspective to that, as illustrated earlier in this chapter, which is argued by Habermas (communicative reason), Gadamer (dialogue), and Ricoeur (conversation-discourse).

62. The work by Whitehead and Whitehead, *Method in Ministry*, has helped shape the understanding of this process as presented in this chapter. They stress three phases: attending, asserting, and deciding.

63. Although Gilbert Ryle was the first to use the phase "thick description," Geertz was certainly the one to popularize it. See Clifford Geertz, *The Interpretation of Cultures* (New York: Basic Books, 1973), 3–30.

64. T. D. Jick, "Mixing Qualitative and Quantitative Methods: Triangulation in Action," *Administrative Science Quarterly* 24 (December 1979): 602–11.

Chapter 6 Spirit-Led Leadership and Organization

1. See, for example, Steven B. Cowan, ed., *Who Runs the Church: 4 Views of Church Government* (Grand Rapids: Zondervan , 2004); and Chad Owen Brand and R. Stanton Norman, *Perspectives on Church Government: Five Views of Church Polity* (Nashville: Broadman & Holman, 2004).

2. Cowan, *Who Runs the Church*; Brand and Norman, *Perspectives on Church Government*.

3. Jim Collins, *Good to Great: Why Some Companies Make the Leap . . . And Others Don't* (New York: HarperBusiness, 2001).

4. Nadler et al., *Discontinuous Change*.

5. Max Weber, *The Theory of Social and Economic Organization* (New York: Free Press, 1947).

6. Frederick Winslow Taylor, *The Principles of Scientific Management* (1911; repr., Mineola, NY: Dover Publications, 1998).

7. Luther Gulick and L. Urwick, *Papers on the Science of Administration* (New York: Institute of Public Administration, 1937).

8. Elton Mayo, *The Human Problems of an Industrial Civilization* (New York: Macmillan, 1933).

9. Chester I. Barnard, *The Functions of the Executive* (1938; repr., Cambridge: Harvard University Press, 1968).

10. James G. March and Herbert A. Simon, *Organizations*, 2nd ed. (1958; Cambridge, MA: Blackwell, 1993).

11. Douglas McGregor, *The Human Side of Enterprise* (1960; repr., New York: McGraw-Hill/Irwin, 1985).

12. Rensis Likert, *New Patterns of Management* (New York: McGraw-Hill, 1961).

13. Chris Argyris, *Intervention Theory and Method: A Behavioral Science View* (Reading, MA: Addison-Wesley, 1970).

14. Ludwig von Bertalanffy, *General System Theory: Foundations, Development, Applications*, rev. ed. (New York: George Braziller, 1976).

15. Philip Selznick, *Leadership in Administration* (1957; repr., Berkeley: University of California Press, 1984).

16. Talcott Parsons, *Essays in Sociological Theory*, rev. ed. (New York: Free Press, 1964).

17. James Thompson, *Organizations in Action: Social Science Bases of Administrative Theory* (1967; New Brunswick, NJ: Transaction, 2003).

18. Paul R. Lawrence and Jay William Lorsch, *Organization and Environment: Managing Differentiation and Integration*, rev. ed. (1967; Boston: Harvard Business School Press, 1986).

19. Daniel Katz and Robert L. Kahn, *The Social Psychology of Organizations*, 2nd ed. (1966; New York: Wiley, 1978).

20. George A. Steiner, *Strategic Planning* (New York: Free Press, 1979).

21. Michael Hammer and James Champy, *Reengineering the Corporation: A Manifesto for Business Revolution* (New York: HarperBusiness, 1993).

22. W. Edwards Deming, *Out of the Crisis* (1982; repr., Cambridge, MA: MIT Press, 2000).

23. Edgar H. Schein, *Organizational Culture and Leadership* (San Francisco: Jossey-Bass, 1992).

24. Karl E. Weick, *Sensemaking in Organizations* (Thousand Oaks, CA: Sage Publications, 1995).

25. Peter M. Senge, *The Fifth Discipline: The Art and Practice of the Learning Organization* (New York: Currency Doubleday, 1990).

26. Margaret Wheatley, *Leadership and the New Science: Discovering Order in a Chaotic World* (San Francisco: Berrett-Koehler, 1999).

27. Bill Gates, *Business @ the Speed of Thought: Using a Digital Nervous System* (New York: Warner Books, 1999).

28. Ron Ashkenas, Dave Ulrich, Todd Jick, and Steve Kerr, *The Boundaryless Organization: Breaking the Chains of Organizational Structure*, rev. ed. (San Francisco: Jossey-Bass, 2002).

29. This approach is found in Hatch, *Organizational Theory*.

30. Ibid., 78–81.

31. Ibid., 127–33.

Chapter 7 Spirit-Led Growth and Development

1. Hatch, *Organizational Theory*, 214–16.

2. Thompson, *Organizations in Action*.

3. Ronald A. Heifetz and Marty Linsky, *Leadership on the Line: Staying Alive through the Dangers of Leading* (Boston: Harvard Business School Press, 2002), 53.

4. This chart is adapted from one developed by the Center for Parish Development (www.missionalchurch.org/). Here, the titles have been changed and the arrows have been adjusted to reflect the discrete character of each type of change.

5. Heifetz and Linsky, *Leadership on the Line*, 14–15.

6. This conception of the cycle of the process of change is based on the seminal work of Kurt Lewin in field theory. His original three phases—unfreezing, intervention, and refreezing—are revisualized and expanded to five phases in this approach.

7. This figure is adapted from Everett M. Rogers, *Diffusion of Innovations*, 5th ed. (New York: Free Press, 2003). Rogers uses five categories. Here the category of late adopters is added, which reflects more accurately what often takes place in institutions like the church, where persons are members rather than employees.

Selected Bibliography

"Ad Gentes Divinitus." In *Documents of Vatican II*. Edited by Austin P. Flannery, 813–56 Grand Rapids: Eerdmans, 1975.

Ahlstrom, Sydney E. *A Religious History of the American People*. New Haven: Yale University Press, 1972.

Allen, Diogenes. *Christian Belief in a Postmodern World: The Full Wealth of Conviction*. Louisville: Westminster John Knox, 1989.

Ammerman, Nancy T. *Congregation and Community*. New Brunswick, NJ: Rutgers University Press, 1997.

Ammerman, Nancy T., Jackson W. Carroll, Carl S. Dudley, William McKinney, eds. *Studying Congregations: A New Handbook*. Nashville: Abingdon, 1998.

Argyris, Chris. *Intervention Theory and Method: A Behavioral Science View*. Reading, MA: Addison-Wesley, 1970.

Ashkenas, Ron, Dave Ulrich, Todd Jick, and Steve Kerr. *The Boundaryless Organization: Breaking the Chains of Organizational Structure*. Rev. ed. San Francisco: Jossey-Bass, 2002.

Banks, Robert. *Reenvisioning Theological Education: Exploring a Missional Alternative to Current Models*. Grand Rapids: Eerdmans, 1999.

Barnard, Chester I. *The Functions of the Executive*. 1938. Reprint, Cambridge: Harvard University Press, 1968.

Barrett, Lois, ed. *Treasure in Clay Jars: Patterns of Missional Faithfulness*. Grand Rapids: Eerdmans, 2004.

Bass, Dorothy C., ed. *Practicing Our Faith: A Way of Life for a Searching People*. San Francisco: Jossey-Bass, 1997.

Bertalanffy, Ludwig von. *General System Theory: Foundations, Development, Applications*. Rev. ed. New York: George Braziller, 1976.

Bevans, Stephen B. *Models of Contextual Theology: Faith and Cultures*. Rev. ed. Maryknoll, NY: Orbis Books, 2002.

Blauw, Johannes. *The Missionary Nature of the Church: A Survey of the Biblical Theology of Mission*. 1962. Reprint, Grand Rapids: Eerdmans, 1974.

Bliese, Richard H., and Craig Van Gelder. *The Evangelizing Church: A Lutheran Contribution*. Minneapolis: Augsburg Fortress, 2005.

Bosch, David J. *Transforming Mission: Paradigm Shifts in Theology of Mission*. Maryknoll, NY: Orbis Books, 1991.

Brand, Chad Owen, and R. Stanton Norman. *Perspectives on Church Government: Five Views of Church Polity*. Nashville: Broadman & Holman, 2004.

Browning, Don S. *A Fundamental Practical Theology: Descriptive and Strategic Proposals*. Minneapolis: Fortress, 1996.

Carey, William. *An Enquiry into the Obligation to Use Means for the Conversion of the Heathens*. London: Hodder and Stoughton, 1892.

Carroll, Jackson W., Carl S. Dudley, and William McKinney. *Handbook for Congregational Studies*. Nashville: Abingdon, 1986.

Chopp, Rebecca S. *Saving Work: Feminist Practices of Theological Education*. Louisville: Westminster John Knox, 1995.

Collins, Jim. *Good to Great: Why Some Companies Make the Leap . . . And Others Don't*. New York: HarperBusiness, 2001.

Corrigan, John, and Winthrop S. Hudson. *Religion in America*. 7th ed. Upper Saddle River, NJ: Pearson/Prentice Hall, 2004.

Cowan, Steven B., ed. *Who Runs the Church: 4 Views of Church Government*. Grand Rapids: Zondervan , 2004.

Cresswell, John W. *Research Design: Qualitative, Quantitative, and Mixed Methods Approaches*. 2nd ed. Thousand Oaks, CA: Sage Publications, 2003.

Deming, W. Edwards. *Out of the Crisis*. 1982. Reprint, Cambridge, MA: MIT Press, 2000.

Dudley, Carl S., and Nancy T. Ammerman. *Congregations in Transition: A Guide for Analyzing, Assessing, and Adapting in Changing Communities*. San Francisco: Jossey-Bass, 2002.

Farley, Edward. *Theologia: The Fragmentation and Unity of Theological Education*. Philadelphia: Fortress, 1983.

———. *The Fragility of Knowledge: Theological Education in the Church and the University*. Philadelphia: Fortress, 1988.

Flannery, Austin P., ed. *Documents of Vatican II*. Grand Rapids: Eerdmans, 1975.

Gadamer, Hans-Georg. *Truth and Method*. Translated by Garrett Barden and John Cumming. New York: Seabury Press, 1975.

Gangel, Kenneth O., and Samuel L. Canine. *Communication and Conflict Management: In Churches and Christian Organizations*. Eugene, OR: Wipf & Stock, 2002.

Gates, Bill. *Business @ the Speed of Thought: Using a Digital Nervous System*. New York: Warner Books, 1999.

Geertz, Clifford. *The Interpretation of Cultures*. New York: Basic Books, 1973.

Grenz, Stanley J. *The Social God and the Relational Self: A Trinitarian Theology of the Imago Dei*. Louisville: Westminster John Knox, 2001.

Gritsch, Eric W. *A History of Lutheranism*. Minneapolis: Fortress, 2002.

Guder, Darrell L., ed. *Missional Church: A Vision for the Sending of the Church in North America*. Grand Rapids: Eerdmans, 1988.

———. *The Continuing Conversation of the Church*. Grand Rapids: Eerdmans, 2000.

Gulick, Luther, and L. Urwick. *Papers on the Science of Administration*. New York: Institute of Public Administration, 1937.

Habermas, Jürgen. *The Theory of Communicative Action*. 2 vols. Translated by Thomas McCarthy. Boston: Beacon Press, 1984, 1987.

Halberstam, David. *The Fifties*. New York: Villard Books, 1993.

Hammer, Michael, and James Champy. *Reengineering the Corporation: A Manifesto for Business Revolution*. New York: HarperBusiness, 1993.

Hatch, Mary Jo. *Organizational Theory: Modern, Symbolic, and Postmodern Perspectives*. New York: Oxford University Press, 1997.

Haugk, Kenneth C. *Antagonists in the Church: How to Identify and Deal with Destructive Conflict*. Minneapolis: Augsburg, 1988.

Heifetz, Ronald A., and Marty Linsky. *Leadership on the Line: Staying Alive through the Dangers of Leading*. Boston: Harvard Business School Press, 2002.

Heitink, Gerben. *Practical Theology: History, Theory, Action Domains*. Translated by Reinder Bruinsma. Grand Rapids: Eerdmans, 1999.

Hoekendijk, J. C. *The Church Inside Out*. Philadelphia: Westminster, 1964.

Hood, Fred J. "Evolution of the Denomination among the Reformed in the Middle and Southern States, 1780–1840." In *Denominationalism*, edited by Russell E. Richey, 139–60. Nashville: Abingdon, 1977.

Hough, Joseph C., Jr., and John B. Cobb Jr. *Christian Identity and Theological Education*. Atlanta: Scholars Press, 1985.

Hough, Joseph C., Jr., and Barbara G. Wheeler. *Beyond Clericalism: The Congregation as a Focus for Theological Education*. Atlanta: Scholars Press, 1988.

Hunter, George G., III. *Church for the Unchurched*. Nashville: Abingdon, 1996.

Jick, T. D. "Mixing Qualitative and Quantitative Methods: Triangulation in Action." *Administrative Science Quarterly* 24 (December 1979): 602–11.

Johnson, Barry. *Polarity Management: Identifying and Managing Unsolvable Problems*. Amherst, MA: HRD Press, 1992.

Katz, Daniel and Robert L. Kahn. *The Social Psychology of Organizations*. 1968. 2nd ed. New York: Wiley, 1978.

Kelsey, David H. *To Understand God Truly: What's Theological about a Theological School*. Louisville: Westminster/John Knox, 1992.

———. *Between Athens and Berlin: The Theological Education Debate*. Grand Rapids: Eerdmans, 1993.

Killen, Patricia O'Connell, and John de Beer. *The Art of Theological Reflection*. New York: Crossroad, 2000.

Kimball, Dan. *The Emerging Church*. Grand Rapids: Zondervan, 2003.

Kotter, John P. *Leading Change*. Boston: Harvard Business School Press, 1996.

Küng, Hans. *The Church*. Translated by Ray and Rosaleen Ockenden. New York: Sheed & Ward, 1967.

Lawrence, Paul R., and Jay William Lorsch. *Organization and Environment: Managing Differentiation and Integration*. 1967. Rev. ed. Boston: Harvard Business School Press, 1986.

Leith, John H. *Creeds of the Churches: A Reader in Christian Doctrine from the Bible to the Present*. Richmond, VA: John Knox Press, 1973.

Likert, Rensis. *New Patterns of Management*. New York: McGraw-Hill, 1961.

March, James G., and Herbert A. Simon. *Organizations*. New York: Wiley, 1958. 2nd ed. Cambridge, MA: Blackwell, 1993.

Marty, Martin E. *Righteous Empire: The Protestant Experience in America*. New York: Dial Press, 1970.

Mathews, Shailer. *Scientific Management in the Churches*. Chicago: University of Chicago Press, 1912.

Mayo, Elton. *The Human Problems of an Industrial Civilization*. New York: Macmillan, 1933.

McGregor, Douglas. *The Human Side of Enterprise*. 1960. Reprint, New York: McGraw-Hill/Irwin, 1985.

Mead, Sidney E. "Denominationalism: The Shape of Protestantism in America." In *Denominationalism*, edited by Russell E. Richey, 70–105. Nashville: Abingdon, 1977.

Middleton, J. Richard, and Brian J. Walsh. *Truth Is Stranger Than It Used to Be: Biblical Faith in a Postmodern Age*. Downers Grove, IL: InterVarsity, 1995.

Mud Flower Collective, The. *God's Fierce Whimsy: Christian Feminism and Theological Education*. New York: Pilgrim Press, 1985.

Nadler, David A., Robert B. Shaw, A. Elise Walton, and Associates. *Discontinuous Change: Leading Organizational Transformation*. San Francisco: Jossey-Bass, 1995.

Niebuhr, H. Richard. *The Purpose of the Church and Its Ministry*. New York: Harper & Row, 1956.

Newbigin, Lesslie. *The Open Secret: An Introduction to the Theology of Mission*. Rev. ed. Grand Rapids: Eerdmans, 1995.

———. *Foolishness to the Greeks: The Gospel and Western Culture*. Grand Rapids: Eerdmans, 1986.

———. *The Gospel in a Pluralist Society*. Grand Rapids: Eerdmans, 1989.

Parsons, Talcott. *Essays in Sociological Theory*. Rev. ed. New York: Free Press, 1964.

Payne, Claude E., and Hamilton Beazley. *Reclaiming the Great Commission: A Practical Model for Transforming Denominations and Congregations*. San Francisco: Jossey-Bass, 2000.

Reeves, R. Daniel, and Ronald Jenson. *Always Advancing: Modern Strategies for Church Growth*. San Bernardino, CA: Here's Life Publishers, 1984.

Richey, Russell E. "Denominations and Denominationalism: An American Morphology." In *Reimagining Denominationalism: Interpretive Essays*, edited by Robert Bruce Mullin and Russell E. Richey, 77–90. New York: Oxford University Press, 1994.

Ricoeur, Paul. *From Text to Action: Essays in Hermeneutics, II*. Translated by Kathleen Blamey and John B. Thompson. Evanston, IL: Northwestern University Press, 1991.

Rogers, Everett M. *Diffusion of Innovations*. 5th ed. New York: Free Press, 2003.

Roof, Wade Clark, and William McKinney. *American Mainline Religion: Its Changing Shape and Future*. New Brunswick, NJ: Rutgers University Press, 1987.

Sanneh, Lamin. *Translating the Message: The Missionary Impact on Culture*. Maryknoll, NY: Orbis Books, 2002.

Schaller, Lyle E. *44 Questions for Church Planters*. Nashville: Abingdon, 1991.

Schein, Edgar H. *Organizational Culture and Leadership*. San Francisco: Jossey-Bass, 1992.

Scherer, James A. *Gospel, Church and Kingdom: Comparative Studies in World Mission Theology*. Minneapolis: Augsburg, 1987.

Schleiermacher, Friedrich. *Brief Outline on the Study of Theology*. 1811; 1830. Translated by Terrence N. Tice. Reprint, Richmond: John Knox, 1966.

Schreiter, Robert J. *Constructing Local Theologies*. Maryknoll, NY: Orbis Books, 1985.

Selznick, Philip. *Leadership in Administration*. 1957. Reprint, Berkeley: University of California Press, 1984.

Senge, Peter M. *The Fifth Discipline: The Art and Practice of the Learning Organization*. New York: Currency Doubleday, 1990.

Smith, Elwyn A. "The Forming of a Modern American Denomination." In *Reimagining Denominationalism: Interpretive Essays*, edited by Robert Bruce Mullin and Russell E. Richey, 108–36. New York: Oxford University Press, 1994.

Stackhouse, Max L. *Apologia: Contextualization, Globalization, and Mission in Theological Education*. Grand Rapids: Eerdmans, 1988.

Steiner, George A. *Strategic Planning*. New York: Free Press, 1979.

Stone, Howard W., and James O. Duke. *How to Think Theologically*. Minneapolis: Fortress, 1996.

Sweet, William W. *The Story of Religion in America*. 1930. Reprint, Grand Rapids: Baker, 1975.

Tashakkori, Abbas, and Charles Teddlie. *Mixed Methodology: Combining Qualitative and Quantitative Approaches*. Thousand Oaks, CA: Sage Publications, 1998.

Taylor, Frederick Winslow. *The Principles of Scientific Management*. 1911. Reprint, Mineola, NY: Dover Publications, 1998.

Thompson, James. *Organizations in Action: Social Science Bases of Administrative Theory*. 1967. Reprint, New Brunswick, NJ: Transaction, 2003.

Thompson, John B., ed. *Paul Ricoeur: Hermeneutics and the Human Sciences*. Cambridge: Cambridge University Press, 1981.

Troeltsch, Ernst. *The Social Teaching of the Christian Churches, Volume II*. 1912. Reprint, Louisville: Westminster/John Knox, 1992.

Trueheart, Charles. "Welcome to the Next Church." *Atlantic Monthly* 278, no. 2 (August 1996): 37–58.

Van Gelder, Craig. "Missional Context: Understanding North American Culture." In *Missional Church: A Vision for the Sending of the Church in North America*, edited by Darrell L. Guder, 18–45. Grand Rapids: Eerdmans, 1998.

———. *The Essence of the Church: A Community Created by the Spirit*. Grand Rapids: Baker, 2000.

———. "From Corporate Church to Missional Church: The Challenge Facing Congregations Today." *Review and Expositor* 101, no. 3 (Summer 2004): 425–50.

———. "Method in Light of Scripture and in Relation to Hermeneutics." *Journal of Religious Leadership* 3, nos. 1–2 (Spring/Fall 2004): 43–73.

———. "The Hermeneutics of Leading in Mission." *Journal of Religious Leadership* 3, nos. 1–2 (Spring/Fall 2004): 139–72.

Volf, Miroslav. *After Our Likeness: The Church as the Image of the Trinity*. Grand Rapids: Eerdmans, 1998.

Volf, Miroslav, and Dorothy C. Bass, eds. *Practicing Theology: Beliefs and Practices in Christian Life*. Grand Rapids: Eerdmans, 2002.

Walls, Andrew F. *The Missionary Movement in Christian History: Studies in the Transmission of Faith*. Maryknoll, NY: Orbis Books, 1996.

Warren, Rick. *Purpose Driven Church*. Grand Rapids: Zondervan, 1995.

Weber, George W. *The Congregation in Mission: Emerging Structures for the Church in an Urban World*. Nashville: Abingdon, 1964.

Weber, Max. *The Theory of Social and Economic Organization*. New York: Free Press, 1947.

Weick, Karl E. *Sensemaking in Organizations*. Thousand Oaks, CA: Sage Publications, 1995.

Welker, Michael. *God the Spirit*. Translated by John F. Hoffmeyer. Minneapolis: Fortress, 1994.

Wheatley, Margaret. *Leadership and the New Science: Discovering Order in a Chaotic World*. San Francisco: Berrett-Koehler, 1999.

Whitehead, James D., and Evelyn Eaton Whitehead. *Method in Ministry: Theological Reflection and Christian Ministry*. Rev. ed. Kansas City: Sheed & Ward, 1995.

Winter, Gibson. *The Suburban Captivity of the Churches: An Analysis of Protestant Responsibility in the Expanding Metropolis*. New York: Macmillan, 1962.

Wood, Charles M. *Vision and Discernment: An Orientation in Theological Study*. Atlanta: Scholars Press, 1985.

Wuthnow, Robert. *The Restructuring of American Religion*. Princeton, NJ: Princeton University Press, 1988.

Zizioulas, John. *Being as Communion: Studies in Personhood and the Church*. Crestwood, NY: St. Vladimir's Seminary Press, 1985.

Index

Craig Van Gelder serves as professor of congregational mission at Luther Seminary in St. Paul, Minnesota, a position he has held since 1998. Previously, he taught at Calvin Theological Seminary in Grand Rapids, Michigan, as professor of domestic missiology (1988–1998). He holds a PhD in missiology from Southwestern Baptist Theological Seminary and a PhD in administration in urban affairs from the University of Texas at Arlington. He is the author of *The Essence of the Church*, editor of *Confident Witness—Changing World,* and coeditor of *The Evangelizing Church* and *The Church between Gospel and Culture*. He has over twenty-five years of experience in working as a church consultant and is presently consulting with Allelon (www.allelon.org) on redeveloping theological education for the purpose of missional leadership formation.

The Essence of the Church: A Community Created by the Spirit

Rather than beginning with successful contemporary models of what churches are doing, *The Essence of the Church* encourages readers to rethink the nature of the church. The author draws on three decades of experience to address the challenges facing today's church and urges readers to think deeply yet practically about the church.

Thoughtful and readable, this book integrates insight from a variety of disciplines and enables readers to root their methods and programs in sound biblical, theological, and theoretical principles. Diagrams help to illustrate the concepts.

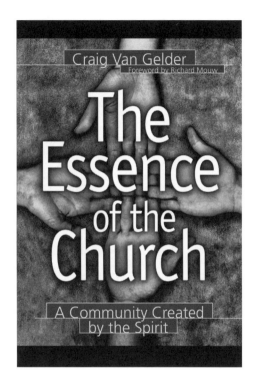

"Wise and necessary guidance. . . . It should be required reading for all who want the church to be faithful to the cause of the gospel in our present cultural context."

—RICHARD J. MOUW, president, Fuller Theological Seminary (from the foreword)

BakerBooks
Relevant. Intelligent. Engaging.
www.bakerbooks.com